# MANAGING THE CONSULTANT

## A CORPORATE GUIDE

# MANAGING THE CONSULTANT

## A CORPORATE GUIDE

JOHN J. McGONAGLE, JR.

CHILTON BOOK COMPANY   RADNOR, PENNSYLVANIA

Copyright © 1981 by John J. McGonagle, Jr.
All Rights Reserved
Published in Radnor, Pennsylvania, by
Chilton Book Company and simultaneously
in Scarborough, Ontario, Canada,
by Nelson Canada Limited
Library of Congress Catalog Card No. 80-68271
ISBN 0-8019-7016-6
Designed by Jean Callan King/Visuality
Manufactured in the United States of America

"Consulting Fees: A Case Study" originally
appeared in *Finance* magazine in slightly different
form. "Commercial Arbitration Rules" and
"Submission to Arbitration" were supplied by the
American Arbitration Association. The publisher
gratefully acknowledges permission to reprint
them here.

1 2 3 4 5 6 7 8 9 0    0 9 8 7 6 5 4 3 2 1

To Carolyn Vella
for her ideas, her inspiration,
her guidance, and her support

2211431

# CONTENTS

**Preface   xiii**

**1. CONSULTANTS AND CONSULTING   1**

**What is Consulting?   2**

   *Management Perspective   2*

   *Legal Perspective   4*

**What Makes Up the Consulting Relationship?   5**

**Do You Need a Consultant?   10**

**Defining the Task   13**

**2. FINDING A CONSULTANT   17**

**How to Find a Consultant   18**

**Consultant Organizations   19**

   *Membership   20*

   *Referrals and Placement   24*

   *Standard and Suggested Forms   25*

   *Standards of Ethics   27*

   *Complaints   27*

   *Disputes   28*

**3. MANAGEMENT ISSUES   31**

**How to Budget for a Consultant   32**

Conflicts of Interest  34

Insurance and Risk  35

Confidential Information  37

Recruiting the Corporation's Employees  39

Recruiting the Consultant's Employees  39

Consulting Fees: A Case Study  40


4. CORPORATE POLICY  45

Why You Should Have a Written Policy on Consultants  46

What Your Policy Should Cover  46

How Other Existing Corporate Policies Affect the Use of Consultants  47

Finder's Fees  48

Outside Independent Public Accountants  50

Outside Legal Counsel and Lobbyists  51

Risk Management  52

Insider Trading  52

Foreign Corrupt Practices Act  53

References  53

Conflicts of Interest  54

Sample Corporate Policy—Preparation of Procedures  54

Coverage  55

Limitations on the Use of Consultants  56

Prior Approval  57

Optional Provisions  58
"Motherhood" Statement  58
Final Report  58
Appraisal and Review  59
Similar Work Clause  60
Budget Clause  60

Consultant Retention Form  61

Sample Letter Confirming Retention of a Consultant  62

Consultant Billing Procedure  63

Consultant Appraisal and Review Form  66

Alternative Sample Corporate Policy  68


5. LEGAL ISSUES  69

Why Legal Issues are Involved in the Consulting Relationship  70

Some Broad Topics That Should Be Considered
in Drafting Consulting Agreements  70

*Services to Be Performed    70*

*Independent Contractor Status; Work*
  *Product; Copyrights and Patents    72*

*Compensation; Costs    73*

*Duration    73*

*Termination    74*

*Restrictive Covenants    74*

*Modification; Nonassignability    75*

*Applicable Law    75*

*Manner of Giving Notice    76*


6.  **THE LETTER AGREEMENT    77**

    **The Difference Between a Letter Agreement and a Consulting Contract    78**

    **Why the Letter Agreement Should Be in Writing    78**

    **Adapting the Letter Agreement to Particular Needs    79**

    *Duration and Services    80*

    *Progress of Work    84*

    *Compensation and Expenses    84*

    *Working Facilities    85*

    *Reports and Work Products    86*

    *Independent Contractor    87*

    *Termination    88*

    *Confidentiality of Information    88*

    *Nonassignability    89*

    *Arbitration of Disputes    91*

    *Integration Clause    92*

    *Closing of the Letter Agreement    92*

    *Description of the Work to Be Performed    93*


7.  **MASTER CONSULTING CONTRACT    95**

    **When an Elaborate Contract is Necessary    96**

    **How to Adapt the Form in This Book    96**

    **What the Contract Should Cover    98**

    *The Parties to the Contract    98*

    *Scope of the Work    98*

    *Work Requests    99*

    *Compensation and Costs    101*

    *Billing Procedure    103*

*Work Product  105*

*Patents and Copyrights  105*

*Confidential Information  106*

*Indemnifications; Limitations of Liability  108*

*Status as Independent Contractor  111*

*Notices  111*

*Equal Employment Opportunity  112*

*Termination  113*

*Assignability  114*

*Subcontractors and Employers  116*

*Corporate Opportunities and Conflicts of Interest  117*

*Insurance  118*

*Applicable Law  119*

*Disputes; Arbitration  119*

*Amendments; Waivers  120*

*Integration and Severability Clauses  121*

**Specialized Contracts  122**


8. **WHEN THINGS GO WRONG  123**

**Why Disputes Arise  124**

**How to Handle a Dispute  124**

**What You Can Sue For  126**

*Damages  126*

*Restitution  127*

*Rescission  127*

*Specific Performance  128*

**Mediation  129**

**Remedies Provided by Agreement  130**

*Liquidated Damages  130*

*Arbitration  131*

**Why Arbitration is Used  131**

**How Arbitration Works  132**


**APPENDIX  135**

**Sample Corporate Policy  136**

*Additional Policy Provisions on Outside Consultants  137*

**Federal Definitions  138**

**Office of Management and Budget Circular A-120   139**

*Guidelines for the Use of Consulting Services   139*

*Attachment   142*

**Consultant Retention Form   144**

**Sample Letter Confirming Retention of a Consultant   145**

*Consultant Billing Procedures   145*

**Consultant Appraisal and Review Form   147**

**Alternative Sample Corporate Policy   149**

**Department of Health and Human Services Policy on Consultant
    Services   150**

*Exclusions   159*

*Congressional Budget Estimate of Consultant Services Guidelines   161*

*Consultant Service Plan   162*

*Project Description and Justification   163*

*Consultant Service Plan Summary Costs Guidelines   165*

*Requests for Consultant Services   166*

*Report on Assessment of Benefits Received from Consultant Services   167*

Guidelines for Preparing Report   167

*Report on Assessment of Consultant Services Rendered   168*

**Letter Agreement   169**

**Master Consulting Contract   174**

**Department of Housing and Urban Development
    Professional Services Contracts   184**

**Fund-Raising Agreement   190**

**Arbitration Clauses   194**

**Extracts from *A Commercial Arbitration Guide for Business People*   195**

**Basic References   200**

*American Arbitration Association Regional Offices   200*

*Consultant Organizations   200*

*Publications   202*

Directories   202
Periodicals   204
References   204

*The U.S. Government and Consultants   205*

General Reference   205
U.S. General Accounting Office   206
U.S. Senate   206

**INDEX   207**

# PREFACE

I wrote this book for any manager who customarily uses consultants or may be thinking of hiring one. The success of a consulting relationship depends on the extent of mutual agreement and understanding between consultant and client. There is no such thing as a standard consulting relationship, not only because each project is different, but also because the relationship between the parties is highly malleable and can be worked into whatever form the parties may choose— or, if they are not careful, into a form that neither has chosen but both are responsible for. When business is presented with such a variable situation, it is useful to have guidelines; and these should be applicable to every level of management.

*Managing the Consultant* is two books in one. It is a basic reference that defines consulting, the client/consultant relationship, and the duties of the parties; explains the roles that corporate policies, contracts, and agreements play in directing the consultant's work; and clarifies the duties of corporate personnel at each executive and management level. *Managing the Consultant* also has a considerable how-to-do-it aspect. Because the contract ought to be the key element in creating and controlling the consulting relationship, I have included contract forms that can be used by the manager or executive as models, or, in many situations, as ready-made contracts. The book explains how to adapt these forms to your situation, and shows the advantages (and, in some cases, disadvantages) of each alternate clause or paragraph. Other forms document corporate policies on hiring consultants, billing procedures, and evaluating the consultant's work.

Although the concerns and problems of non-profit organizations and government bodies are different from those of private business, their circumstances as consumers of consulting services should be the same; therefore, the principles and contracts contained here are appropriate for use by any organization, whether private or public.

# CHAPTER ONE

# Consultants and Consulting

## WHAT IS CONSULTING

### Management Perspective

The diversity of the consulting industry is remarkable. Consultants are found in virtually every field. There are consulting engineers, one of the oldest sectors of the consulting business. There are accounting firms, which provide management consulting services. There are management consulting firms, which provide executive and employee recruitment and compensation services. There are advertising firms, which provide media consulting services. There are political consultants, who advise individuals on how best to get elected. There are firms that provide consulting to the giant corporations of the world on the very essence of their business, finances, marketing, and personnel. And then there are firms that provide the most specific kinds of advice to the narrowest submarket, such as consulting firms that specialize in providing advice on the acquisition, merger, and dissolution of law firms only.

Where consultants appear and how often they appear is almost impossible to list. When we look at the materials put out by and about the giant management consultants and when we read the advertisements and talk with the people who provide the consulting services on their own, we quickly realize that consulting may be the most diverse and most broad-based business in America today. Consultants advise America's and the world's great corporations on the creation of new products and may assist in their actual development. They often aid competing companies to evaluate similar questions of strategy and tactics in current and future marketing strategies. They assist giant banks in selecting future financial markets and how banks can best position themselves to deliver future services. They provide expertise to companies who wish to improve productivity. They also provide expertise to companies who wish to participate in the political process, offering business perspectives to lawmakers in the hope of effecting legislative change.

In the government, consultants are very often at the right hand of policy makers, providing studies and advice. Critics of the federal government's consulting procurement process have asserted that very often the consultants themselves are the policy makers, serving without the control of the agency and not subject to congressional supervision or confirmation.

These same policy consultants bring their expertise to the private sector, indirectly constituting another connection between government and industry. This connection may be insidious, seen by many as another revolving door where industry can influence the government and can learn its policies and inner workings before policies are formally established. Another perspective is to see the consulting industry as one way the government controls the economy. By helping to formulate policy and by being privy to the policy-making process, the consultant who then advises the private-sector company or individual of the long-range goals, strategy, and tactics of government is, in a way, regulating that business by his advice. The consultant who can tell the head of a major company the direction a particular government agency is heading controls that company perhaps as surely as the government lawyer who writes regulations that will be binding on that company.

Consultants are a tremendous source of research. For this reason, it is not surprising that many consultants have come from America's academic community. In fact, many members of that community serve as part-time consultants. Stories are rife of academics whose part-time consulting business provides a greater income than their full-time teaching position; stories also point to situations where the so-called part-time job occupies more time than full-time teaching. This has led some universities to consider limiting such outside work, on the theory that dedicating substantial amounts of time to paying clients will cause academics to neglect their teaching and research on campus. This trend could mean that academics with heavy consulting commitments may find themselves cut off from the very faculty position that provides the exposure and prestige that brought them the business in the first place.

In addition to providing a product, consulting firms often provide a process. The consulting industry provides studies and advice on marketing, cash flow management, data management, storage, transportation, telecommunication, and many other processes related to the final output of an institution. Very often these processes dominate the activities of the institution, so that by providing guidance the consulting firm may, to an extent not realized by all parties, be setting the ultimate direction of the institution.

Consultants also provide direct services. They advise individuals in the political process, steering potential candidates through the intricacies of federal and state election laws. Consultants also may suggest the most effective way to seek to influence legislation.

Consulting and the consulting business have been subject to less analysis than ridicule. One definition of the process of consulting comes from *The Devil's Dictionary,* in which Ambrose Bierce defines the verb "consult" thus: "to seek another's approval of a course already decided upon." A well-known joke defines a consultant as someone who when you ask him what time it is takes your watch, reads it for you, and then leaves with your watch. A third definition, which has been circulated in many civil-service circles, is that a consultant is anyone with a briefcase more than fifty miles from home.

The concept of the consultant can be approached from either a management-services or legal perspective. From a management-services perspective, consultants are often used by organizations, whether in the private or public sector, to provide outside assistance from time to time for a variety of reasons. Some of the most commonly cited reasons are the following:

**1.** There is a shortage of expertise among existing staff and personnel, and the nature of the work being done does not warrant the hiring of full-time personnel, even for a temporary appointment. Many consulting firms offer a concentration of specialties that make their use a relative bargain.

**2.** There is a shortage of staff, usually because of hiring restrictions in government or personnel and budgetary restrictions in private business. Many contracts are let to consultants because the consultant can provide management not available at the time to the organization hiring the consultant.

**3.** There is a shortage of time. This is often a variation of the above rationales when a given task or project must be performed quickly and the corporation's section charged with completing the project is unable to meet the demands placed upon it without outside assistance.

**4.** There is a need for an "objective" or "outside" point of view. Corporations and government agencies often are so enmeshed in their own problems or so limited in their institutional perspectives that they feel the need to bring in fresh ideas to provide insight, guidance, or a solution to a current problem.

For ease of discussion, the institution hiring a consultant henceforth will be called the corporation, although individuals and governments also hire them. The term consultant will be used whether the consultant is a partnership, an individual, a corporation, or a university.

## Legal Perspective

It is instructive to view the many attempts made to define a consultant. Most have been undertaken by the federal government, which from time to time engages in efforts to limit the use of consultants, to control the role of consultants in policy-making functions, to keep consultants from managing the execution or implementation of government programs, and to keep consultants from being hired when they may be placing themselves in a conflict of interest.

Although the definitions are many, each reflects an attempt on the part of a government agency to define a consultant in terms of other management or control objectives. Thus, one government agency may define a consultant broadly to permit it to hire consultants, while another agency may define a consultant narrowly so that it is not prevented, by conflict of interest regulations, from hiring consultants for a needed project. Congress may define ''consultant'' in its very broadest and most generic sense in order to provide uniform legislation governing the employment and use of consultants; the Office of Personnel Management may distinguish a consultant from a temporary employee for certain personnel and management purposes.

The Appendix contains a number of definitions of consultants used or proposed for use by the federal government. They are included to provide examples of definitions for use in corporate policies and for reference when drafting consulting agreements.

From a review of these definitions and from similar definitions in the private sector, the conclusion is that a consultant provides consulting services and consulting services are provided by a consultant. This definition is not as circular as it seems. Clearly, a consultant is different from an employee, an agent, or a partner. But it is just these distinctions and differences that are critical, from the legal perspective, to the existence of the consultant. It is only by understanding the management role of the consultant that one can understand the necessity for clarifying the consultant's legal status. The legal status of the consultant is an unusual one, one that clothes the consultant with certain restrictions from the point of view of management. For example, the American Institute of Architects (AIA), in dealing with the architect-consultant relationship, notes that generally a consultant's services and responsibilities derive from the agreement between the architect and the owner, making the consultant subject to these terms and conditions. The architect, in the eyes of the AIA, has overall responsibility for administering a project, entitling him or her to retain consultants of his or her own choosing.

## WHAT MAKES UP THE CONSULTING RELATIONSHIP?

Given the disparate approaches to consulting and the fact that the consultant is a creature of the modern business and industrial world, to understand what a consultant is it is necessary to understand the legal nature of the consulting relationship. Fundamentally, the status of consultant is conferred only by the agreement between two parties; there is no such thing as a consultant as a matter of law.

The consulting agreement, in widespread use today in both the public and private sectors, is a bastard child of the employment contract and the contract that has created the independent-contractor relationship, frequently found in the construction field. In the case of the employment contract, also called a contract of service, traditionally the employer selects the employee, is responsible for payment of wages, establishes compensation, provides direction, controls the employee's method of doing work, manages the work place, and supervises or dismisses the employee. With these managerial prerogatives come legal obligations arising out of a whole complex of legal notions encompassed under the phrase "employment relationship." These obligations include the following:

Agency: When an employer hires and supervises an employee, the employee acts only in the employer's interests. Although subordinate to the employer, the agent can bind the employer legally.

Vicarious liability: The damages an agent or employee inflicts on others are the responsibility of the employer. The employer, not the employee, must compensate the victim of the employee's mistakes.

Regulation of the work place: Employers are required to provide safe work places for employees and worker's compensation insurance to compensate injured workers for business-related accidents or illnesses.

Under the classic independent-contractor relationship, on the other hand, an employer hires an expert or specialist to do a certain task but retains no supervision or daily control over how the expert accomplishes that task. This means, among other things, that the employer has no direct control over the specialist's own employees. In this way, the employer is insulated from certain legal and managerial liabilities in exchange for relinquishing certain managerial prerogatives. The reasons for entering into this relationship, which is basically like the consulting relationship, are varied. Several reasons are commonly advanced and are close to the reasons usually given for hiring a consultant. The reasons most often given are the following:

1. Limited or one-time use of specialized skills.
2. Unique areas of expertise.
3. Limitations on corporate wage scales.

4. The unavailability of specific skills in a current labor market.
5. Rapid access to the latest technology and experience in its application.
6. Multiple exposure to alternative solutions to new problems.
7. Credibility as an outsider.
8. Limitations on executive time.

In general, the consulting agreement falls between the contract of service, or the employment relationship, and the contract for services, or the independent-contractor relationship. It is substantially closer to the latter than to the former but has elements of each. For example, the corporation receives the services of an expert or specialist but does not surrender all managerial or supervisory powers. Rather, the consultant is placed in the status of an independent contractor with the corporation, but the parameters of the consultant's task may be subject to continuing definition or modification by the corporation as the task proceeds.

As a result of this unique power to intervene in the handling of the task contracted to the consultant, the consulting agreement, which creates the consulting relationship, includes many of the elements found in the traditional employment contract but also some critical independent-contractor elements appropriate to such a hybrid relationship.

In light of the special nature of the consulting agreement and consulting relationship, several key topics should be handled in management's creation of the consulting relationship and ultimately in the preparation of the consulting agreement. The topics elemental to every consulting relationship include:

1. nature and scope of the services to be performed
2. status as an independent contractor, including handling of the work product
3. payment of compensation and costs
4. duration of the relationship
5. termination of the relationship
6. modification of the relationship and the work to be performed
7. restrictive covenants to protect the corporation
8. settlement of disputes and interpretation of duties, compensation, etc.
9. remedies upon default or failure to perform
10. manner of giving notice, changes in assignments, etc.

These topics are dealt with in chapter 3 from a management point of view and in chapters 5, 6, and 7 from a legal point of view.

Because of the complexity of these elements of the consulting relationship and consulting agreement, the relationship never should be entered into orally. In fact, it may be virtually impossible to create and enforce an oral consulting agreement. The chief problem in such a relationship is a point of law known as the statute of frauds, which provides, in broad terms, that an oral contract is void if by its terms it cannot be performed within one year after the contract is made. A 1970 decision by an appellate court in New York is instructive in this regard. In this case, a man alleged that he was to be employed by the Corning Glass Works for the period May 1, 1966, through April 30, 1967, as a management consultant, for a fee of $25,000. The agreement was an oral contract entered into based upon discussions that took place in February and March 1966. The appellate court, in a brief opinion, ruled that this agreement was void, since by its terms it was not to be performed within one year of its making, even though the alleged term of the contract was only one year.

Even if a contract is originally oral and falls within the statute of frauds, the enforceability of any renewal may be affected by the statute. For example, the renewal of a written contract for a period of employment of one year for another year requires a written memorandum, even though each separate contract is within the applicable one-year statute of frauds. The application of this statute to the consulting relationship is particularly critical. Many consultants are hired on an intermittent basis or are hired for one project and then hired again to continue with another element of the same project; other consultants are put on a retainer by a corporation, to be used from time to time. Both of these agreements, whether partially or wholly oral, run substantial dangers of being void and unenforceable.

Many people believe that by merely calling an individual a consultant, he or she becomes a consultant. To a degree, this is true. In preparing any agreement between a consultant and a corporation, the hiring organization never should be termed an employer, as this designation could be used to undermine the contention of either or both parties that the consultant is, for the purposes of the agreement, an independent contractor. This is critical, as the wrongs of an independent contractor cannot be attributed back to the person who hired the independent contractor. Stipulating in a consulting agreement that the consultant is an independent contractor vis-à-vis the corporation does not automatically create the independent-contractor relationship. The failure to make this statement can be held against the parties, but a stipulation that the parties have this relationship is a good starting place.

By establishing that the relationship between the corporation and the consultant is that of an independent contractor, the corporation is giving up the right to direct and control the consultant and the consultant's employees, both in the outcome and in the manner and means by which that outcome is obtained. This is the essence of the independent contractor-consultant relationship. The corporation must respect this allocation of control, as in a lawsuit the court will look beyond the language of the agreement to the actual conduct of the parties in order to determine their true relationships. For example, if a court must decide whether the wrongs (torts) of a consultant are the responsibility of a corporation, which presumably has substantially greater assets to pursue, the court will not stop at a document. If the court determines, based on facts, that the corporation has been exercising control over the consultant or the consultant's employees, including the manner and means in which the work assigned to the consultant is being conducted, the court may find that, despite the language of the agreement, the relationship is that of employer to employee. This then would subject the corporation to what is known as "vicarious liability" for the torts of what would be deemed "borrowed" employees, meaning that although the consultant and his employees working on the project are not on the payroll of the corporation, they are presumed to have been loaned to the corporation or borrowed by the corporation. In that case, the corporation can be sued for any torts committed by them.

Another critical element in determining what a consultant is is the ability of management to control the nature of the task. That is, the corporation must be able to modify the task from time to time without impinging upon the manner in which the task is accomplished. For reasons of the statute of frauds and because of the dangers of attributing the wrongs of a consultant's employees to the corporation, all modifications of the agreement and relationship, including specific instructions and directions, always must be in writing. Modifications and instructions may cause problems with both the statute of frauds and the need for the consultant's duties to be specific. If the parties are careful and make such directions in writing, they have provided protection from a legal point of view as well as a management point of view.

Thus, we have come full circle. A consultant provides consulting services, and consulting services are provided by a consultant. It is clear that a consultant is not an agent, nor is a consultant a partner or a joint venturer or an employee. A consultant is not merely an independent contractor but is closer to an independent contractor than to any other traditional legal form. As the consultant is a nontraditional creature of the law, extreme care must be taken from both a legal and management point of view to provide that the relationship is clearly established, maintained, and terminated. Within the concept that the consultant is one who is retained to provide advice, the consulting relationship can and should be the creation of a mutual understanding of two parties. Beyond that, there is no such thing as one exclusive definition of a consultant. A consultant is one person or institution who provides particular advice to another person or institution but who is not internal management, a regular employee, a partner, or a contractor. In order to establish that a consultant is none of these, the parties must define clearly what a consultant is. Without a clear understanding by the parties involved—incorporated in written policies, budgetary controls, and agreements— the consultant relationship will not exist, and the courts, in any lawsuit, will tend to treat the relationship as one more familiar to them: employer-employee, partners, etc. This means that the legal relationship between the corporation and the consultant, as well as their relationship to third parties, will differ, perhaps radically, from what the corporation and the consultant intended. It cannot be stressed too strongly that if the parties do not establish their relationship in writing, then the courts will establish one for them, one that may not be acceptable to them.

Ultimately, just as management science has come to view the consultant as an ordinary, necessary, and reasonable adjunct to the process of business and government, so too will the law tend ultimately to accept the consultant as a separate legal entity with separate legal rights, responsibilities, and obligations. Until that time, parties entering into a consulting relationship carry the risk that the relationship does not exist unless they carefully and clearly define it; they also enjoy the advantage that they can make the relationship what they want to make it when they want and for the purposes they want. Being an evolving legal concept, the ambiguities can be dangerous or beneficial. From a management point of view, too, the ambiguities present opportunities as well as perils. If the parties work together to define the nature of the relationship and the need for the kinds of services sought, the relationship will work to their mutual benefit and satisfaction. If the parties are unable to answer the legal questions, they most likely will be unable to answer the management questions. Clear thinking in one area reflects clear thinking in another.

## DO YOU NEED A CONSULTANT?

The first step in determining whether you need a consultant is to define the problem. Defining the problem is not as simple as it may seem. Before the decision to hire a consultant is made, the following questions must be answered:

What is the issue?

What needs to be done? Is it a process or an ultimate goal?

What, because of financial capacity or regulation, cannot be done?

What does the corporation want as the end product of a consulting relationship?

What does the corporation need as the end product of a consulting relationship?

What operations will be affected by an attempt to solve the perceived problem?

How quickly must the problem be resolved?

What resources are available in terms of personnel and money?

The definition of the problem is not a task that should be left to upper management alone. Rather, all levels of management affected by the perceived problem should be consulted before seeking other information. Upper management, middle management and line employees see problems from different perspectives and may see solutions that one of the other levels is unaware of. It is conceivable that the process of defining the problem may result in an internal solution.

If the corporation is unable to determine the nature of the problem or lacks the specialized resources to make an accurate assessment, it can retain a consultant to evaluate the nature of a problem and recommend the kind of a specialist or specialists necessary to solve it. The result of this decision may be the preparation of what is known as a Request For a Proposal (RFP). The RFP is a device often used by government and one which is, quite frankly, not popular with consultants. An RFP normally asks potential bidders to evaluate a problem and state how they would solve it, what methodology they would use, how much time it would take, and what the approximate cost would be. The reason consultants do not like this system is that in the competitive bidding common to RFPs, the consultants are investing time, effort, and money with no guarantee of receiving a contract. From the point of view of the corporation, it may be a way to better define the problem and to make a more efficient use of limited resources when retaining and selecting appropriate consultants.

In reviewing the problem as it has been defined by the corporation, the next question to be asked is whether the corporation is facing an issue of strategy or of tactics. That is, is the question "should we?" or is it "how?" Some corporations will not seek or be receptive to outside advice on matters of strategy, preferring to hire outside assistance for tactical decisions only. Other corporations feel very strongly that they are capable of generating a decision but need advice as to an overall strategic course to adopt. In evaluating the nature of the problem, the corporation should face this issue squarely.

Having defined the problem, the corporation should then determine who best can solve the problem as stated, outside consultants or inside employees. The benefits and reasons for employing outside consultants were mentioned briefly above. There are other issues, pertaining to the operation of the corporation itself that may affect the decision to use current employees or an outside consultant. Employees, for example, may have a vested interest in asserting that no problem exists. On the other hand, an outside consultant may have a bias toward solving the problem in the one particular way it has solved similar problems in the past. From another perspective, the decision to go outside of the corporation may have a discouraging effect upon employee morale if such a decision is seen as a vote of no confidence in the ability of employees to solve the problem or to honestly evaluate its cause. In the extreme, some employees may see the decision to hire an outside consultant as a conclusion that they are the cause of the problem and that the solution will mean their dismissal, demotion, or lack of promotion.

In some situations, an outside consultant may be retained in order to give credibility to the obvious solution to the problem. It is often much easier to sell an unpalatable solution to senior management and/or a board of directors if it is proposed by an outside consultant than it is to sell the same solution if proposed internally.

A final issue involved in the determination of whether to employ a consulting firm is the question of the relationship between the corporation and the consultant. If a corporation is seeking advice as to its activities in a new field, it must expect that it will be engaged in a long term commitment of capital and labor. If it hires an outside consultant at the beginning, this may mean that the corporation will be making a long term commitment to the consulting firm. On the other hand, if decisions are made internally, the corporation has not tied itself on a long term basis to a consulting firm or firms.

When the decision to hire a consultant has been made, there are several traps to avoid. The first trap is telling the consultant (directly or indirectly) the solution. The consultant is hired to bring expertise to the problem. If you make clear what you think the solution should be, you may well expect the consultant either to decline the assignment or to come up with the solution you want, rather than the solution you may need. Another trap is to completely defer to the judgment of an expert in the field. When hiring a consultant well-known in a particular area, management must realize that the consultant is providing advice. Management should not abdicate its judgment-making abilities and accept, point-by-point, the recommendation of an outside consultant without a careful evaluation.

A slightly different trap lies in management's response to the consultant's needs. There is a substantial danger that management, in the belief that it has carefully defined the problem, will not give the consultant the opportunity to redefine the problem as work progresses. The most extreme example of this is when the corporation limits the consultant's access to individuals or operations within the corporation in the belief that the consultant doesn't need certain information. The consultant can only work with the information it receives. If the consultant is screened from potentially important contacts, the value of its ultimate product will be diminished.

## DEFINING THE TASK

In initial discussions with potential consultants, the corporation should begin by presenting the problem or assignment directly to the consultant. That a consultant understands the problem and says that it can solve it is not enough. Although the corporation may feel limited in evaluating the ability of the consultant (because it cannot solve the problem itself), there are several items that the corporation should discuss in order to decide whether to retain a particular consultant. These include:

General information on the consultant and his or her experience.

Specific information on key individuals employed by the consultant who would be working on the project. It cannot be overstressed that the corporation, if it is hiring individuals with particular experience, should always assure itself that these individuals will be the ones working on its particular problem.

The consulting firm's experience in similar areas. With whom has it had this experience? What solutions has it created for other clients similarly situated? What was the cost/benefit ratio of the solutions proposed? Did its clients accept and implement the solutions?

Is the strength of the consultant in the strategic or in the tactical solution of problems?

What references can the consultant provide, other than clients or completed projects?

Are the individuals to be assigned to the corporation's project the same individuals who have worked on similar projects for other corporations?

The corporation should feel free to compare one consultant with another. Some of the large international consulting firms produce material describing their corporation, operations, particular strengths, and recently completed projects, which can serve as a guide for a corporation seeking to evaluate competing claims of expertise.

Having made a preliminary assessment of the consultant and his ability to deal with the problem as the corporation has defined it, the corporation should then engage in another level of analysis. The first is to present an RFP to the consultant, if appropriate. If the consultant is still under consideration for the project, but it has become clear that the corporation's perception of the problem appears to be somewhat in error, it may be useful to ask the consultant to prepare an RFP.

Additional topics to be covered at this stage include the question of how the project will be assigned within the organization, the experience, abilities and background of the individuals to whom it will be assigned, and how the project will be supervised and controlled. In addition, the corporation should determine how the consultant will provide additional manpower, if that is necessary, to work on the project.

The parties should discuss openly exactly what the consultant will need from the corporation, covering not only fees and costs, but also the commitment of the corporation's own resources, including the time of key executives and employees. The corporation should determine whether it is willing and able to commit key individuals, in a potentially overworked environment, to dedicate substantial amounts of time to the project. If the corporation is unable or unwilling to do this, then the nature of the task to be performed by the consultant may change radically.

Further specific details to be discussed can cover issues that ultimately will be included in the final agreement between the parties. One such issue deals with the disposition of work papers prepared by the consultant. The need for careful thought here is illustrated by a case reported in the *Washington Post*. A private research firm had received a contract to conduct clinical tests of a drug on which the U.S. Government had already conducted laboratory tests. The clinical tests were necessary to get FDA approval to sell the drug. The consulting firm's contract provided that it would keep the data it gathered and ultimately would get the exclusive rights to sell the drug if FDA approval were granted. During the term of the contract, the Department of Health, Education and Welfare (HEW) attempted to rewrite this contract and asked the consultant to give up its future rights to the drug. The consultant declined to do so and HEW refused to continue the contract. Although it had paid the consultant, HEW never obtained any of the completed clinical tests, because the contract did not provide for this.

Before any work is begun, the parties should decide whether the corporation wants one solution or a series of alternatives. The corporation should also determine and make clear what kind of cost/benefit standards, if any, it expects to be applied to the solutions proposed. A solution which is financially impossible for a corporation under its current financial structure is no solution at all.

A trap to avoid, and one difficult to perceive, is the purchase of consultants with a prepackaged solution. In such cases, the consultant will be very assertive, pointing to similar problems which it has solved for other companies. The corporation should be particularly careful to note whether the solution to all of these problems appears to be the same. If it does, then the consultant is selling a product (its prepared solution) and not a process (an answer to your problems). A final point to discuss is the question of reporting. Management should be particularly wary of the consultant who indicates that he or she will take a project and report back at the end of the term but does not feel the need for ongoing status reports, progress meetings, or other forms of monitoring communication.

# CHAPTER TWO

# Finding a Consultant

## HOW TO FIND A CONSULTANT

As in finding an employee, where you find a consultant depends in large measure on where you want to look. In seeking a consultant, a corporation may be subject to constraints not present in hiring an employee, so its experience in that area is not immediately transferable. A chemical company, for example, may not want to advertise that it is seeking a consumer-goods marketing consultant; its current competitors may be able to deduce future marketing strategies from this fact. For this reason, it may be difficult to check a consultant's credentials, particularly one who has worked for competitors. Further, employees may be disturbed to learn that the corporation is seeking a consultant skilled in reducing personnel cost.

Despite these constraints, direct advertising is not out of the question. Governments and educational institutions advertise for consultants; there is no reason why business cannot do the same.

More traditionally, consultants can be located through a combination of the following techniques:

Refer to existing corporate consultant evaluation reports

Survey key employees for leads

Review membership lists of consultant associations

Research trade press for discussions of activities of consultants working in similar areas

Check advertisements in industry publications

Check library services for published papers or articles on related topics

Place open or blind advertisements

Each of these sources will turn up names of individuals and organizations. The search does not end there. The diligent executive must expand the list creatively before limiting it. Individuals identified with a consulting firm two years ago may now be with another firm; this new firm also may be a candidate. A large consulting firm identified with a major government contract covering issues similar to those under study by the corporation may have subcontracted specific portions of the contract to more specialized firms; these firms should be added to the list.

In soliciting names of consulting firms, the corporation should be careful to avoid the trap of the "old, established firm." Just because a firm is large and has been around a long time does not make it the best qualified. For reasons of efficiency and equity, the corporation should seek less well-known firms. Being smaller, they may be more responsive; being newer, they may be more aggressive; being specialized, they may be more economical.

Failing to search for the newer, smaller firm can have legal ramifications. As federal set-aside and affirmative-action programs put more money into minority businesses, minority consulting firms will grow in number and experience. The corporation that fails to accord them fair consideration someday may face a suit for racial or sexual discrimination.

Once having assembled a list of potential consultants, the corporation must proceed to evaluate them. The corporation should contact the targeted firms and seek a statement from them as to their qualifications to undertake an assignment and their ability to consider assuming the assignment. The firms should be advised of any threshold limitations, such as their ability to perform within a certain period of time or to work at a specific location. The statement of qualifications and interest then can be reviewed to determine which firms should be contacted for further discussions. These discussions can be as elaborate as interviewing each firm or asking each firm to submit a complete bid and project description, or they can be as simple as sending a contract to one firm and asking if they will sign it and begin work.

## CONSULTANT ORGANIZATIONS

When I had to find organizations of consultants, I turned to the Encyclopedia of Organizations. This annual publication lists and indexes thousands of voluntary organizations by name, areas of principal interest, and geography. Its index does not show consulting as a profession or occupation; instead, organizations of consultants are listed according to fields of specialization, including engineering, management, and communications.

Rather than checking with every possible area of interest, I scanned the listings for every group that identified itself with consulting by its title. I then reviewed the summary of each to determine if its membership included active consultants. From this group of about thirty-five organizations, I chose ten. They varied widely in size, age, and the specializations of their members. This random selection was designed to elicit as representative a sample as possible.

In addition to these names, I obtained the membership list of the National

Council of Professional Services Firms. I selected this group because of its active involvement in efforts to amend the federal government's procurement regulations concerning consultant services. This organization is made up of eight separate organizations.

My search produced a large list of organizations, all of which were identified with consulting and all currently active. This list included organizations of management, personnel, agricultural, fund-raising, political, nursing, and engineering consultants.

I sent each organization the same letter, asking a few basic questions about the organization. The responses varied. Letters to two organizations were returned by the Postal Service. Three other organizations did not respond to my inquiry. One personnel consulting association sent a list of its members, usually sent to executives seeking to change positions. The balance answered the questions, generally by forwarding materials with a covering letter; these organizations responded to most of the questions, and several responded to all of them.

This experience shows that even after you identify organizations of possible use, you cannot expect all of them to reply. And of those that do reply, not all will respond to your precise concerns. Most organizations contacted did answer, however, and were both coöperative and useful.

The tables on pages 22 and 23 and discussions summarize the results of this survey. The discussions do not identify the specific organizations, as they are intended to illustrate the variety of activities and resources that organizations have and you may be able to use. By knowing what these organizations do, you will know better what to expect from other organizations.

## Membership

Membership qualifications of course vary widely, depending on the purpose of the organization. Every organization that responded to the inquiry had some sort of membership qualifications. The employer of consultants can view these qualifications from several angles. One angle is to determine whether the qualifications identify or isolate consultants whose experience and abilities are relevant to the project at hand. Another angle is to study the qualifications of an organization whose members you already regard as competent to do the job; in this way you can determine if there are standards it uses to evaluate potential members that you can apply to persons who are not members of these organizations.

One organization indicates that its membership is by invitation only after a

thorough investigation of qualifications, experience, and local reputation, followed by a personal interview with a firm already a member of the organization.
Membership in this association is limited to one member firm from each designated marketing area. Evaluating this, a purchaser of consulting services must
rely on the reputation of the organization or of consultants whom they know are
members. In the latter case, reputation is being acquired by transference. Limiting
membership to a particular area should tell the potential purchaser of services
that a future referral will yield only one or two members per locale. A review of
the qualifications indicates that members are not limited to servicing clients in a
particular area, so a potential purchaser of consulting services should make
inquiries of all members of this association.

Another organization has a different set of qualifications for membership.
This association requires that applicants be interested in the field in question and
have their financial responsibility and business experience established. Such
individuals are eligible for membership as nonprofessionals. Full membership
requires that applicants, in addition to these qualifications, have a college degree
or documented equivalence in the discipline involved, have completed a one-day
written examination, and have submitted previous work products from the field.
Membership is then available to those with at least two or five years of experience, depending on the membership category. The standards are more objective
in this organization, but the only ones usable outside of this organization in addition to actual experience (presumably an important factor with many consultant
retentions) are the facts that there is a college degree or the equivalent available
in this field and that this association emphasizes education.

A third organization serves as a certification organization and identifies itself
as such. Certification standards provide a guide to a corporation attempting to
evaluate consultants in general, as well as consultants in its particular field. This
association requires that, to obtain certification, the applicant must have had at
least five years' full-time experience in the specialty in question and during that
time must have had major responsibility for client projects. Applicants must provide references, half of which must be from executives or clients represented in
the previous five years. These references are investigated to assure that the
client relationships were satisfactory. The applicant also must provide written
summaries of several client assignments, protecting the identity of the client. At
least one of these must describe in detail the nature of the problem, the purpose
and scope of the assignment, the analytical approach used, the solution recommended by the applicant, and the results achieved by the client. This project sum-

| | Membership Qualifications | Referral Service | Ethical Standards | Enforcement | Handles Complaints Against Members | Standard Forms | Dispute Resolution |
|---|---|---|---|---|---|---|---|
| American Association of Fund-Raising Counsel, Inc. | yes | directory | yes | expulsion | no | — | no |
| American Consulting Engineers Council | yes | directory; informal | yes | expulsion | no | yes | no |
| American Council of Independent Laboratories, Inc. | yes | directory | yes | expulsion | informal | no | informal |
| American Management Associations | yes | directory | no | no | informal | no | no |
| American Society of Agricultural Consultants | yes | directory | yes | — | — | no | — |
| American Society of Appraisers | yes | directory | yes | expulsion | formal | no | informal |

| Organization | | | | | | | |
|---|---|---|---|---|---|---|---|
| Association of Consulting Management Engineers, Inc. | yes | directory | yes | expulsion | no | — | — |
| Association of Productivity Specialists | yes | informal | yes | no | informal | no | informal |
| Independent Computer Consultants Association | yes | yes | yes | expulsion | informal | yes | mediation |
| Institute of Management Consultants, Inc. | yes | — | yes | expulsion | — | — | — |
| National Association of Merger and Acquisition Consultants | by invitation | yes | yes | expulsion | informal | no | arbitration |
| National Society of Professional Engineers | yes | directory | yes | expulsion | no | yes | no |
| Society of Telecommunications Consultants | yes | directory; informal | yes | expulsion | informal | no | — |

mary is considered vital by the association. Following this are interviews with current members to establish the applicant's professional competence.

Although membership in this association may give a potential client confidence, its usefulness is limited to certification only. Still, the steps the association has gone through to certify the consultant can serve as a model for a potential client seeking to retain a consultant, at least in the final stages of an interview or retention process.

A fourth organization, in an engineering field, relies heavily on direct experience and state licensing. All potential members must be licensed to practice and must practice in the engineering field. Although not all consultants are licensed, a firm seeking to retain consultants should consider whether the consulting services can be provided in whole or part by licensed individuals. Using licensed individuals may permit the client corporation to evaluate their abilities better, at least by establishing that the individual is currently licensed and has not been subject to any disciplinary actions by a licensing board. A potential client should not rely solely on this, as it involves the abdication of responsibility and sound business judgment to a licensing board. Merely because a project *can* be performed by someone licensed does not always mean that it *must* be performed by someone licensed. Reviewing the standards for licensing may give a client corporation additional ideas and bases for evaluating potential consultants in terms of their objective abilities and past experience.

## Referrals and Placement

Almost every organization responding had some kind of referral service, either formal or informal, enabling nonmembers to get in touch with members of the association. These services range from informal to highly elaborate directories. In many cases, the service simply enabled nonmembers to have access to a directory of members. The availability of directories from organizations is noted in the organization references listed in the Appendix, but the safest course is to inquire directly of the organizations if such a directory is available, what it includes, and whether there is a charge for it.

One organization indicated that inquiries for services available from its members are received regularly at its headquarters and are answered by the association. As there is no indication that it has a directory or membership list available, this referral service is conducted by the staff at the association's office only. Another organization indicated that its central office served as a referral center, sending a membership directory to anyone wishing it. The directory costs about five dollars and consists of two parts, a list of members and an index by geographical location, which refers to specific pages. Each page describes the company or individual and the services provided. Obviously designed by the member, the listings are little more than detailed, full-page advertisements. In spite of this, the information provided is substantial and may be useful to a potential consumer. Users of this and other directories should take great care to ascertain if the summaries of membership abilities and qualifications have been prepared by the members themselves or if they have been compiled on some more objective basis by the organization.

A third organization indicated that it was currently in the process of setting up a system whereby it would be able to refer potential clients to members with expertise in the area that the potential client has identified. The nature of this system was not described, but the organization wrote that it currently supplied a membership roster to interested individuals or firms; this roster does not indicate specific skills of members, however.

A fourth organization has an elaborate directory containing substantial information on its members. The manual is arranged with each entry under the principal headquarters of the member, by state, and is cross-indexed by the name of the firm. The description of the firm includes such facts as its size, names of the principals or partners, a brief description of the firm's activities, whether the firm is public or private, and if it is a subsidiary, who the corporate parent is. No price for this directory is indicated. It is published annually.

With any referral service lists or directories, the corporation should be careful to note the date of publication. Some organizations do not print directories regularly; relying solely on the directory even to contact current members can result in many newer, smaller, and potentially more aggressive firms being omitted from a search. It is usually a good idea to contact the association after reviewing its directory to find out if there are any members who are not included. If so, obtain information on them and add it to the inventory of potential consultants.

## Standard and Suggested Forms

Of the organizations contacted, only three indicated that they had prepared and made available to their members any standard forms. One organization stated that it had a standard form contract available to members, but it suggested that its members check with their own lawyers in any special situation; this form presumably is not available to nonmembers for review. A second organization, with engineering members, had an extensive list of contract documents governing particular construction problems; the documents were prepared by a committee representing this organization and two other organizations and are available to nonmembers as well as members at a nominal charge. The organization encourages their use for the benefit both of the consultant and the client. The organization noted that there is a substantial advantage in using standard documents and contracts containing carefully prepared language to define the responsibilities of the parties. It also advised, however, that all these documents have important legal consequences and should be reviewed by the member's legal counsel.

A third organization that indicated it had forms available to the public participated in the publication of the forms through the joint committee mentioned above.

The subject of standard forms is very important. The Appendix contains suggested forms, both contracts and management policy statements. Over time, these documents can be molded to fit the needs of the client corporation. Standard form contracts for the provision of professional services or consulting services serve the same purpose. From the point of view of the client corporation, it is useful to know that such contracts are provided to members even if they are not available to nonmembers, for this increases the likelihood that the consultant it may be dealing with will propose his organization's standard form contract as a beginning point for negotiations. Even if a potential client is not familiar with the form contracts, knowing that a standard form will be proposed gives the client a perspective on the bargaining over the terms of the agreement.

The standard form agreement prepared by an organization gives you a significant advantage for several reasons. First, you will be aware that the consultant may propose that the relationship be entered into based upon this standard form. Second, if the consultant uses the standard form, you will be familiar with it and will understand what it intends to do, having had time to review it. Third, if the consultant has developed his own form, that form likely will reflect many of the standard clauses in the organization's form. Fourth, by reviewing the contract forms you can evaluate your own agreement to determine whether there are problems unique to this industry that should be reflected in your agreement; you then have the opportunity to modify your agreement to make it apply more specifically to this industry before entering into negotiations for the acquisition of consulting services. Finally, studying standard contract documents enables you to understand better how the consultant works within a particular industry. Understanding how consultants work will enable you to deal with them and utilize their services more effectively once you have entered into a legal relationship with them.

## Standards of Ethics

With one exception, every organization responding indicated it had a code of ethics or professional standards applicable to its members. These standards cover professional behavior, confidentiality of client information, use of the designation of membership in the association, and a wealth of administrative matters covering both internal operations of the organization and relations of its members to their clients and the public.

A key issue, however, is whether and to what extent these organizations have established a mechanism for enforcing these standards of ethics upon their members. Enforcement mechanisms for ethical standards vary widely. One of the large organizations, containing people from virtually all of the management sciences, has no mechanism to assure compliance with its standards of ethics. One of the smaller organizations indicated that all members must agree to abide by the association's code of ethics or forfeit membership. Another organization of engineers enforces its code of ethics through an elaborate series of disciplinary procedures. These procedures include a hearing; an investigation by the organization; and a variety of disciplinary actions, including unpublished or published censure, investigation, and disciplinary action, suspension, or termination of membership. Here, too, the ultimate discipline to be imposed for a violation is expulsion, although the organization does realize that its corporate members may wish to impose sanctions upon its own employees, officers, or directors.

Another organization established formal investigative processes to deal with allegations that members have violated its ethical standards. Included in these procedures are limits on the length of time within which the investigation can be conducted and a provision that formal charges need not be filed by an injured party but that the party must be willing to provide substantiating evidence or forfeit the investigation. The same standards apply as before; that is, the ultimate sanction is expulsion.

## Complaints

Two areas in which organizations may be engaged in activities of interest to the client pertain to whether the organization receives complaints from those who employ its members and how these complaints are handled. A similar issue is whether the organization aids in settling disputes between its members and non-members through mediation, conciliation, arbitration, or otherwise. In many organizations, these questions are related to the ethical standards. One organization, for example, when asked about both professional ethics and complaints against its members, indicated that they were treated as questions pertaining to the ethical code , which was enforced through an ethics committee. At that point presumably the complaint either is handled through the regular enforcement procedures or dismissed on the grounds that it did not constitute a violation of the organization's code of ethics.

Another organization clearly separated its ethics enforcement function from the question of complaints, noting that it had a committee to deal with professional ethics and grievances. This committee responded to complaints of unethical professional practices of members.

A third organization handled complaints from corporations that retained its members quite differently. It indicated that it handled these complaints routinely and informally through its office, since they were mostly nonexistent.

Another organization, separating enforcement of its ethics code from complaints, indicated that its ethics committee also handled complaints against its members, regardless of the fact that they did not pertain directly to violations of ethical standards. It did not indicate how these complaints were handled by the organization once they were received.

The general pattern seems that most organizations do not have a procedure for handling complaints against their members apart from their professional or ethical standards. To the extent that they do, the receipt of complaints is handled formally; the complaints are reviewed to determine if they allege any violation of the ethical standards of the organization.

## Disputes

The associations all were asked whether and to what extent they entered into the settlement of disputes between their members and nonmembers. Here the answers were the most varied. One organization indicated that its board of directors was available and "competent to adjudicate complaints and mediate disputes between members and nonmembers"; this association noted, however, that during the past three years no such instance had occurred. Although many organizations did not answer this question, the response they might have made probably would be similar to this one.

Another organization noted that it had adopted a slightly different method of handling complaints. It likened its handling of complaints to that of the Better Business Bureau; that is, it attempted to mediate disputes but candidly noted that, except for expelling a member, it had no recourse to enforce the resolution of a dispute.

A third organization noted that it aided in disputes between members and nonmembers by making arbitration available. Finally, one organization indicated that as a trade organization it cannot legally become involved in any disputes. This last statement alludes to a sensitive area in dealing with organizations in general. In recent years, the U. S. Department of Justice has sought to place the activities of professional and trade associations under the federal anti-trust laws. The position of the federal government has been that organizations often use codes of ethics and enforcement procedures, including expulsion, as a way of fixing prices or engaging in other anticompetitive practices.

In general, in recent years, the courts have limited the penalties available to organizations to fines, suspension, and expulsion, generally removing from organizations the power to impose other penalties, such as economic boycots or the withholding of commercial or trade information from its members. The courts have held that as trade organization disciplinary boards are similar to courts, members of these organizations must be provided with certain minimal procedural protection. From the point of view of the nonmember who wishes to make a complaint about a member of the organization, this means that the complaint must be one that can be prosecuted by the complainant. Procedural safeguards allow the member being charged to cross-examine his or her accuser so that the accuser cannot remain anonymous.

Given the concern of the Department of Justice with anticompetitive effects of codes of ethics and disciplinary processes, anything seen to have the effect of fixing prices so as to prevent competitive bidding is illegal. This means that the nonmember company cannot hope to obtain help from the organization if a member has violated some element of the ethical code pertaining to pricing practices.

# CHAPTER THREE

# Management Issues

## HOW TO BUDGET FOR A CONSULTANT

One of the most ignored areas in dealing with consultants is the problem of bud-geting for consulting services. To many, the concept of budgeting for consulting services seems an anomaly. How can one plan to hire individuals or companies to perform services that have not even been determined and to provide answers to questions that may not have been asked? Although this sounds as if it is impossible to budget for consultants, the same objections can be raised about budgeting for almost any service. In thinking about consulting services, a corpo-ration should be guided by several principles.

These principles are derived from sound management and common sense. First, how much money has the corporation spent on consulting services in the past? If the corporation has retained consultants formerly, this can serve as a benchmark. Many corporations will be surprised to find that they do not know how much money they have spent on consulting services. Sound management requires that they determine this, for one of the first steps in controlling an issue is to determine its scope.

Second, the corporation should determine which projects it foresees in the coming fiscal year. Those corporations with long-range planning systems should be aware of new projects under consideration. These projects may be as narrow as salary review or as broad as acquisition or divestiture. In any case, reference to a long-range plan will provide a guide to budgeting for consulting services.

Third, the corporation should look to see what fundamental changes are being made elsewhere in its budget. A corporation in the midst of imposing a personnel freeze may find it will exert pressure on its executives to utilize con-sulting services to replace the services that formerly had been provided inter-nally. Conversely, the corporation that expects to increase its personnel by add-ing new employees or by adding new business units may determine that the future need for consulting services will drop, not rise.

The mere act of asking each unit that prepares a budget to think about this issue may bring forth some fairly surprising answers. As indicated above, it may give to management for the first time a clear picture of the extent of consulting services it uses. It may disclose to management deep-felt needs that have not had other ways to come to the surface. Regardless of the manner in which it is approached, budgeting for consulting services is no more mysterious a process than budgeting for raw materials, increased personnel costs, or income in various fields. It requires a consistent frame of reference, so that all participants are asked the same questions to provide consistent answers for management planning. As with any other management tool, the way in which budgeting is structured can predetermine its outcome. Few examples of budgeting procedures for major corporations are available, in part because budgeting and financial planning strategies are among the most closely guarded procedures of corporations today. This also reflects the fact that many corporations do not consciously budget for consulting services but rather take consultant services out of personnel, overhead, or miscellaneous budget categories. In particular, those budgetary systems that permit managers to transfer funds relatively freely from one category to another will not generally see middle-range management coming forward affirmatively with estimated budgets for consulting services. Consulting services in these circumstances are covered by the ability of management to reach into other funds; in this way, management can continue to view the purchase of consulting services as a contingency to be covered out of a surplus in the budget rather than as a line item to be planned, just as raw materials, insurance, and sick time are planned.

Due to the confidentiality of corporate budgeting processes, the only models available are those of the government. The U.S. Department of Health and Human Services (formerly the U.S. Department of Health, Education, and Welfare) has a chapter in its general administration manual that outlines a consulting services policy. (The chapter is included in the Appendix.) In addition to dealing with the acquisition and management of consulting services through the government's procurement system, this policy attempts to deal with budgeting for consulting services. The policy presumes that consulting services are used by many elements of the department, on a recurring basis and as a regular, as distinguished from extraordinary, tool of management. If anything, the guidance provided is geared towards an organization that may overuse rather than underuse consulting services.

Read with this understanding, it can be seen that the Department of Health and Human Services manual treats consulting services as any other budgetable item. Each unit is asked to estimate its needs for consulting services and to justify the kinds of consulting services it expects to acquire during the next fiscal year. Because of the long time involved in establishing and procuring a federal budget, the planning process for consultants for any fiscal year begins at least seven months earlier.

The budget and consulting service system designed by the Department of Health and Human Services is geared to a review of consultant service purchases as a group rather than to a review of the justification of an individual contract. In addition, it reviews certain consulting services after the fact rather than before the fact. Read with these restrictions and policy directives in mind, this policy, as bureaucratic as it is, provides one of the rare insights into the management of consulting services. Its prime lesson is that consulting services can be budgeted and administered like any other services acquired by any business or government agency.

As discussed earlier, this policy contains many of the key elements any corporation should consider in establishing its own policy on consulting services. It defines what consulting services are, with an understanding both of the services to be performed by consultants and the manner in which this organization will use consultants. It describes how consulting services are to be acquired and managed on a regular basis. It establishes the terms under which consulting services are acquired and sets restrictions on the ability of the managers involved to modify the contract signed with the consultant. Finally, in addition to a budget-cycle preparation, it requires the user of consulting services to assess the services provided. To that degree, it is a relatively complete model of a corporate policy. What must be understood is the direction this policy takes. It is designed for a large government organization working within a rigid budget and subject to specific procurement regulations, which must justify its activities after the fact rather than before the fact. Still, it provides a model for management because it raises the fundamental issues that management must address. What is most helpful is that it raises the budget issue as a part of the other management issues discussed in this chapter.

## CONFLICTS OF INTEREST

The question of conflicts of interest is raised in the next chapter in terms of receiving assurance from consultants that their activities do not constitute a conflict of interest with their principal employer. In preparing a conflict-of-interest policy, the corporation should be aware that its employees can serve as consultants to another business, which may place the employee in a conflict of interest. More specifically, conflicts may arise in the classic situation where the outside business' operations compete with an activity of the corporation, but they may also occur when the outside business has dealings with the corporation and the employee has a material, proprietary interest in that business. A third concern is that an employee's outside interest may subject him to unreasonable demands upon his time that could affect his primary job adversely. To put it bluntly, the outside job may keep him from performing adequately for his primary employer.

A conflict-of-interest policy should address these issues, especially since many people engage in part-time consulting activities. A corporation also should think through carefully whether the business interests of a member of its employee's immediate family could constitute a conflict of interest. Here the danger is in creating an overly broad policy that attacks too much, one result of which is that compliance will fall off sharply as employees ascertain what they believe to be inherent unfairness and overreaching on the part of the corporation. For example, employees may determine that a corporation's policy is inherently unfair when it prevents them from engaging in any outside employment if it can be interpreted to bar them from public service or civic activities for which they are paid.

Also related to this is the question of nepotism. More and more, corporations are drafting policies on employing, promoting, or transferring relatives. Originally, most companies did not permit hiring relatives. Now, with the increasing number of marriages in which both partners are working, companies have found it useful to employ both husband and wife in order to make job transfers easier and to permit rapid advancement of one or both spouses. Those corporations with policies prohibiting the employment of relatives should decide whether employment means merely full-time salaried individuals or whether, as with the federal government, they are attempting to encompass consultants employed on a long-term basis. That is, they may wish to assure themselves that no corporate consultant employs a close relative of any corporate employee, either on a particular project or at all. If this is the corporation's position, the employment-of-relatives policy should spell this out. The consultant should be made aware of this in the early stages of negotiations so that he may check within his organization to prevent an accidental violation of this policy.

## INSURANCE AND RISK

Although it may seem that the status of the consultant as independent contractor should eliminate any insurance considerations, at least as far as the corporation is concerned, this is not the case. As indicated in more detail in chapter 5, the fact that the independent-contractor relationship has been established will not prevent it from being attacked. Injured employees of the consultant may sue the corporation on the theory that the corporation ultimately was their employer if the consultant has not been carrying the legally required limits of worker's compensation coverage. Or the consultant's employees may sue the corporation not as employees but because the corporation exercised control over their assignments and therefore should be responsible for any injuries to them. From either point of view, the corporation should be concerned with the insurance coverage of the consultant's employees to protect itself both directly and indirectly.

Worker's compensation insurance is not the only issue to be considered by the corporation. Various insurance contracts that the corporation has in force may extend coverage to classes of individuals without the corporation's knowledge. For example, an accident policy extending travel accident coverage that covers persons "actually in the employ" of the corporation may extend to independent contractors as well as traditional employees. In addition, some companies may carry a form of industrial policy in the nature of liability insurance that covers its employees for a monthly premium based upon the number of individuals employed. In such cases, even though the parties regard the consultant and the consultant's employees as independent contractors, the insurance policy may regard these individuals as covered workers, so the corporation has to pay for this coverage.

Other insurance issues include the question of professional liability. As discussed in chapter 7, a corporation may wish to assure itself that the consultant it employs is carrying insurance sufficient to protect it from future damage suits. In cases where third parties sue for harm they have suffered, the corporation may wish to look to the consultant to contribute some or all of the damages due to the consultant's participation in the project that led to the lawsuit. The corporation also may wish to assure itself that its consultants have sufficient insurance covering general liability losses, so that if the corporation suffers injury there is compensation available should its action against the consultant be vindicated.

The corporation should realize that its individual directors and officers may be held to answer for the selection of the consultant. This area is emerging only recently but is of increasing concern to the business community. It is not improbable that some day officers and directors of a corporation may be sued personally for negligence in retaining a consultant or for failure to supervise a consultant, as a result of which a third party has been injured. In this regard, a careful review of the directors' and officers' liability insurance, also called errors and omissions insurance, is in order. To the extent that the coverage demands that certain decisions be carefully documented, the rationale for the selection of a consultant and the manner in which he is selected may be subject to stringent written requirements.

A collateral area is the rising concern with white-collar crime. Although theft, particularly theft not covered by insurance, is not generally regarded as an insurance issue in lay terms, theft losses are increasingly important. Corporations no longer are strictly concerned with the theft of hardware or cash. In this modern era, computer time and information itself are commodities that can be stolen and resold profitably. In bringing a consultant into its operations, a corporation must realize that the opportunities for white-collar crime are increased, not because consultants are more negligent or venal than the corporation's own employees but because more opportunities are created for more people to have access to more valuable information, services, and goods. As a part of any sound risk-management program, the corporation should review its own internal-security precautions to make sure they have been designed to accept the intervention of outside consultants into the corporation's activities. In this regard, the corporation should consider the scope and extent of its fidelity bond before retaining a consulting firm that will have access to valuable records, goods, or money. In the past, fidelity bonds generally covered specific employees or specific positions. In the modern business world, many believe it is more efficient to write fidelity bonds on a blanket basis, covering most or all employees of a company to protect a corporation against losses from dishonest or fraudulent acts. The corporation retaining a consultant should consider expanding its fidelity bond to cover the consultant and the consultant's employees. This is often difficult, in which case the corporation, in those sensitive situations when it is clearly justified, should require the consultant's employees to be covered by a fidelity bond by an insurance company acceptable to the corporate employer. These are not fidelity bonds required by law but fidelity bonds that both parties contractually agree should be purchased to cover their respective liabilities.

## CONFIDENTIAL INFORMATION

In working with a consultant, a critical issue is the consultant's access to the corporation's information and how the consultant will handle this information. This is discussed in part in the previous sections on insurance, risk management, and white-collar crime, as well as in conjunction with some basic contractual provisions set forth in chapter 5. Access to information is a pervasive problem, one that the corporation and consultant must face almost daily. To perform effectively, in many cases the consultant must have direct, continuing, and unimpeded access to certain corporate records and information. In some cases, the consultant must have access to information of a level of detail and sensitivity usually made available to only the most senior executives in the corporation.

The issue is not merely protecting the confidentiality of the employer's information while the project is ongoing, but in some cases protecting the employer's information from being disclosed within the corporation itself. To be specific, in some corporations compensation levels are an extremely sensitive subject but certainly no trade secret. The consultant working on employee compensation problems may have access to figures showing the compensation of every employee and executive of a corporation. The corporation may not be concerned if the consultant reveals this information to a third party, as it had the foresight to protect against such disclosure in the contract; the corporation probably will be concerned, however, if this information is revealed elsewhere within the corporation. Such an issue should be discussed clearly and carefully with the consultant before the agreement is signed, for internal disclosure may be even more sensitive than external disclosure.

A related concern is confidentiality after the agreement has ended. In the agreement, the parties usually have provided that the consultant may not reveal confidential information obtained from the corporation. This does not prevent the consultant from advertising that he has worked for the corporation in question. Some consultants will list previous well-known clients; others will summarize work they have done but mask the identity of the client. Some corporations may not wish to disclose the fact that they have hired a consultant of a particular expertise. A corporation that is revamping its inventory controls in order to move into new lines of endeavor may not wish to see its name displayed as one of the clients of a consulting firm that specializes in inventory control and materials handling; such advertising could telegraph a message to the competitors of the corporation. The corporation may wish therefore to inform the consultant that its name may not be disclosed for a fixed period of time, regardless of whether the disclosure entails revealing confidential information or not. Restrictions on the consultant should not be imposed unnecessarily, as the consultant's ability to perform for future clients may depend upon his ability to refer to the services performed for past clients. In essence, the consultant builds upon the reputation of his clients, since he cannot specify in detail the work that has been performed.

Often a consultant, in identifying his expertise and experience, describes specific projects he has performed for clients. Although these projects may be couched in extremely general terms, competitors may be able to discern the identity of the employing corporation from the description of the project involved, when it was performed, or by reference to other continuing corporate relationships between the consulting firm and the corporation. Obviously, the sensitivity of these data diminishes as time passes. But a corporation concerned that its competitors know it has retained consultants also may wish to discuss such kinds of representation and advertising seriously with its consultants. The corporation should realize that in limiting the consultant's ability to make general reference to such projects, it may be rendering its contract less profitable to the consultant and may have to pay extra for the privilege of removing such descriptions from the consultant's materials. The corporation wishing to prevent either of these disclosures, direct or indirect, of its business relationship with a consultant should remember that this may be damaging in the long run. The corporation seeking to evaluate a new consultant may ask for a description of past clients and past assignments. Corporations that prevent their former consultants from disclosing such information make it harder for them to get new assignments; when other corporations also follow such patterns, they make it harder for them to evaluate new consultants. This is where too much of a good thing can hurt the corporation.

## RECRUITING THE CORPORATION'S EMPLOYEES

One management issue not always appropriate for inclusion in a contract is the transferability of employees. Occasionally, employees working on a particular project for a corporation may seek to work for the consultant in the future. An agreement prohibiting the consultant from hiring employees of the corporation is onerous and possibly unenforceable. Narrowly drawn and aimed at certain employees, an agreement that the consultant not hire away those employees for a limited period of time due to their participation in the project may be enforceable. Such an agreement, however, may have very restrictive and undesirable effects on the corporation and its employees.

## RECRUITING THE CONSULTANT'S EMPLOYEES

The consulting firm has a related problem, one that the corporation should be sensitive to. A consulting firm may agree that it will not work for a competitor of the corporation for a fixed period of time following the termination of the contract. Unless the consulting firm has written agreements with its own employees, however, there is no way it can prevent them from working for a competitor of the corporation or for a consulting firm who in turn works for a competitor. As employees of the consultant, they are bound by the consultant's agreements to respect corporate confidentiality and protect trade secrets. If the corporation is deeply concerned about the dissemination of confidential information, it may wish key employees of the consultant to be bound by the confidentiality clauses in the contract. As in the case of binding its own employees, the corporation should be extremely careful in its insistence on such a clause, for this may demonstrate a lack of trust in the integrity of the consulting firm. The corporation that insists on such a clause should be prepared to justify it and to keep its impact as narrow as possible.

## CONSULTING FEES: A CASE STUDY

It may be a revelation for the company to learn how its assignment is handled and how fees are determined. The following is a brief illustration of these issues. In this example, the firm retained is an outside law firm. Lawyers, of course, are also consultants; the corporation will find that many of the large management consulting firms it retains are structured and operate like large law firms.

When a law firm is hired, the corporate executive communicates with a senior partner in the firm, or with a middle-line partner who is responsible for his corporation's work assignments. After a brief discussion of the problem, the partner refers the assignment to a partner of less seniority, entailing another conference. The associate who is working on the matter will enlist the services of one or more junior associates, each of whom may receive only a portion of the assignment.

In part, this pyramidal system is used for reasons of efficiency: the project may, in fact, easily be divided into discrete units, each of which can be worked on separately under the supervision of more senior associates. Perhaps as important for the law firm, the system also serves to train the junior associate by having him or her work on small pieces of larger assignments, with the work reviewed and revised further up the pyramid. Consequently, the work will be farmed out in the interest of providing on-the-job training, even if the senior associate can do it just as efficiently himself.

This learning process also involves the presentation of the work product of the junior associate to the senior associate, his review and feedback on the work, revision by the junior associate, additional editing, follow-up research or drafting, integration of this product with the other portions of the assignment, and final review. The senior associate then makes his presentation to the partner, who, in turn, may integrate it with other projects, or simply review it. The finished product is returned to the assigning partner, who also reviews it, often by calling for an oral briefing. This attorney then presents the work to the client.

The work at each level is not done with the same expertise, nor do the attorneys spend equal amounts of time on their portions of the assignment. Inasmuch as many law firms bill their clients for the work done on a "straight hourly" basis, it may be helpful to understand how this process works. Each attorney (partner and associate) keeps time records upon which regular reports are prepared, reflecting, in fractions of an hour, the time spent on work for each client and, in some cases, on each separate matter for each client. Each associate is told to record all time spent working on matters for every client, and to let the partners determine whether the client will be billed for that time.

In most large firms, there is the additional pressure to produce a high level of billable hours because they have become an important measure of profitability. The modern law firm operates on a rule of thirds for the time spent by associates: one-third of the time spent will be billed to cover their salaries; one-third will cover their share of the firm's overhead; and one-third will be their contribution to the profits of the firm. There is little incentive to discount the time put in by associates, since any discount will reduce profits directly.

The partners of the firm regularly review the total time recorded for each client, and prepare the bill accordingly. Often the bill will reflect the time spent at its full value—including, on occasion, time spent by a junior associate who worked unnecessarily in one area before being stopped by his supervisor (the superfluous work would be listed as "research"). Further, the learning process is built into this matrix and will be reflected in the final bill.

To illustrate: a firm receives an assignment that can be done adequately by one senior associate. If the work is performed by the various layers of the organization, the calls, conferences, research, reviews, and revisions may result in a total elapsed time of 7 hours and 45 minutes. Were the senior associate to do the work, the total amount of time would be 4 hours and 30 minutes, or about half the time of the junior associates. (For reasons of ethics and liability, his work would be reviewed and then transmitted, adding 1 hour and 40 minutes.) Assume that the rates for the attorneys are as follows: senior partner, $100 per hour; junior partner, $75 per hour; senior associate, $50 per hour; junior associate, $25 per hour. (These rates are supposed to reflect the ability and efficiency of the attorneys involved; the senior associate receives twice the rate of the junior associate, and it is presumed that he works on the assignment twice as fast.) At these rates, the time shown on the firm's books for the assignment handled in the traditional manner would be $665, and for the assignment handled only by the senior associate, $350.

One rule to be learned from this example is to establish who is actually doing the work, and to communicate directly with that person. A corporation will save money by doing this. The firm's practice of reviewing the work as it progresses up and down the pyramid should also be discussed. The learning process and some of the review is purely for the benefit of the firm. The corporation should pay only for the work needed. Although the differences in rates among attorneys may accurately reflect their comparative efficiency, they do not compensate for the review and learning process. Unfortunately, the general figures used internally by the law firm, as well as those provided to the client, can unintentionally mask mistakes and inefficiency. The associates are urged to report all the time taken on behalf of a client; the partner preparing the bill may have no idea whether the time spent at the lower levels was proper or excessive. His natural tendency will be to bill most or all of the time reported at the normal rates established by the firm. This can be particularly insidious if the firm is doing substantial amounts of work for the corporation. For protection, the corporation should ask the law firm to open a new billing entry for each project or request, and also ask to have the bill broken down by assignment and date. In this way, the matters upon which excessive amounts of time were lavished can be isolated, and the billing partner will be able to discount the time instead of billing it at the full rate. The names of the attorneys who worked on the matter should also be shown on the bill. A single assignment that involves a large number of people may be more expensive due to the inherent costs involved in transferring it from one attorney to another. When one attorney replaces another, he or she may have to review the files and the work in progress to get up to date. This time is recorded and could show up in the bill.

By requesting that each project be itemized and billed separately, the costs of the various assignments can be evaluated. One result might be that routine service can be provided by outside counsel at a lower cost. Another might be a request that the law firm charge a standard fee for recurring matters. Comparisons can also be made between bills for similar services rendered at different times; a bill that is excessive in comparison to prior bills bears investigation.

The corporation should also find out who actually does the work. Many firms have administrative assistants, or para-legals, who handle certain routine matters and report their time to the firm, which adds it to the attorneys' time at a lower rate. Generally, this time is included in the total for "legal services." If such work is stated separately on the bill, the corporation can determine whether the work should be given to the law firm or be handled internally. Also, this information may permit the corporation to present the assignment to the law firm at a different level, thereby avoiding several costly steps in the pyramid.

Some law firms will hire an outside legal consultant for very specialized problems, such as patent, copyright, or admiralty law. Some firms merely include the cost for such work in the total for legal services, leading the client to believe that its law firm is doing the work when, in fact, those specialized questions are being handled elsewhere. Such costs should appear as a disbursement, identifying the lawyer to whom the fee was paid, so that the corporation can judge whether it is efficient to send these problems to its general counsel or directly to the specialist. Remember, each time a new attorney is introduced, the assigning counsel may charge for the transition time. The new counsel will also bill for that time, and may then have to review the corporation's files and general operation, billing for that time as well.

The law firm sells its time. When you ask an attorney to do something, the firm's meter begins to run. Every phone call costs money. Every business lunch your attorney takes you to costs you both the meal and the attorney's time. When you ask an attorney to travel, remember that you are generally charged for his trip on a door-to-door basis. Thus, if your attorney flies to your Chicago office from New York for a four hour meeting, you will pay for his time from the departure from his office (or even his home) in New York to your office, even before he begins to work, and for the return trip as well, even if he has no work to do on the return leg (unless he can fill this time with work for other clients). A short four hour meeting in Chicago can cost you twelve hours of lawyer time.

Disbursements and their control should also be considered. If an attorney or his secretary works late, they may be paid for dinner, for cab fare home, and, in the case of the secretary, for the overtime at higher rates. You should isolate these costs and determine how common they are and why they occur. They can reflect a high-pressure, over-worked environment at the law firm or your own habit of not contacting counsel until the last moment. Also, find out what standard, if any, the law firm uses to charge these costs to clients. For example, if the attorney worked on other business during the day and on your business at night, are you charged for these costs? Should you be? Remember, the pressure on a consulting firm is to bill out as much of its direct expenses as possible. Knowing this should enable you to ask the right questions.

# CHAPTER FOUR

# Corporate Policy

## WHY YOU SHOULD HAVE A WRITTEN POLICY ON CONSULTANTS

One of the biggest problems facing any company using consultants is controlling their hiring and use. Most corporations have no policy on the hiring and use of consultants, usually because consultants can be used in so many different areas that management never perceives the need for an overall policy on consultants.

With no policy, a corporation has no control, except budgetary, over the services consultants provide. Without control, a corporation can neither guarantee that the consultants are being used most effectively nor adequately protect its own interest in such areas as trade secrets.

With a policy, a corporation has control. The very process of creating a policy is an assertion of control and an exercise in sound management. In creating a policy, management must decide what consultants can do, what they should do, what problems they can cause, and how they should be hired.

A written policy is better than an understood policy for several reasons:

An understood policy can become misunderstood over time, either through misinterpretation or mistakes in transmitting it to new managers

A written policy can be reviewed by all affected managers before it is put into place so that it meets their needs more adequately

A written policy can be modified more efficiently than one that is merely understood. As is said in the military, someone always fails to get the word

A written policy does not necessarily mean that consultants will be hired and managed uniformly, but it does permit uniform retention and management standards.

## WHAT YOUR POLICY SHOULD COVER

The contents of a corporate policy on consultants should reflect the structure and operation of the corporation. In spite of the necessity of reflecting unique conditions, such as decentralized management, a basic corporate policy should cover at least the following topics:

The responsibility for preparing procedures governing the retention and use of outside consultants and consulting services covered by the policy

Overall limitations on the proper use of consultants, such as whether they are counted against personnel limits

Whether prior approval to hire a consultant is necessary and, if so, by whom

Additional topics often included in written policies on the retention and use of outside consultants deal with the following:

Requiring that all consultants agree to be bound by the corporation's policies

Requiring that the consultant's final report be sent to a particular individual in the corporation

Establishing a system of approval and review of the performance of outside consultants

Requiring the disclosure of similar work done by other consultants for the corporation

Requiring that the retention of all outside consultants be reported when prior approval of their retention is not necessary

Providing for budget control over the projected use of consulting services in the future

## HOW OTHER EXISTING CORPORATE POLICIES AFFECT THE USE OF CONSULTANTS

Without being overly broad, there is virtually no corporate policy that does not have some impact on the retention and utilization of outside consultants under some set of facts. For example, a corporate policy on reimbursement for travel and entertainment expenses may, by its very terms, apply only to employees. Yet sound management dictates that it should apply to consultants as well, for several reasons:

It establishes a complete set of standards

It may reflect tax considerations, so that reimbursements not in accord with it may not be tax deductible

It may damage employee morale to know, for example, that consultants can travel first class while they can not

In general, all existing corporate policies should be reviewed to determine the following:

Do they now apply to outside consultants? If not, should they? How? If they do, should consultants be exempted?

Should they be modified to reflect the status of the consultant compared with the employee?

How best can consultants be made aware of the existence, limits, and application's of company policies?

There are a number of areas where experience has shown that the corporation should consider establishing new or amending existing corporate policies to address the problems raised by the retention and use of consultants:

Finder's fees

Outside independent public accountants

Outside legal counsel and lobbyists

Risk management

Insider training

Foreign Corrupt Practices Act

References

This list illustrates the variety of areas that should be considered. The policies each corporation has will vary, reflecting its history, businesses, and regulatory environment. Even if a corporation does not have or need policies in these areas, it should review all corporate policies to establish whether they should be revised to cover the acquisition and use of outside consulting services.

## Finder's Fees

An area in which many corporations have no written policy but instead an oral policy or set of standards is in dealing with finder's fees in conjunction with mergers and acquisitions. Many merger and acquisition transactions are conducted with the assistance of business-merger consultants retained by the corporation. They advise corporations on potential acquisitions, including suggesting possible merger targets and evaluating the benefits and detriments of potential deals. They also may assist in the negotiations leading to an acquisition. For these specialized services they may be paid a fixed fee, an hourly rate, a contingent fee based on the acquisition price, or some combination of these.

There are also business-merger consultants who attempt to broker acquisitions on a free-lance basis. That is, they approach potential merger partners suggesting that a particular company is a good takeover target. They are "finders." In such cases, the business broker or merger consultant may perform a useful service to a corporation in identifying future investments. These brokers who act as finders can claim a fee by reason of the existence of an implied or oral contract with the corporation they contacted. A critical problem arises when such information was unsolicited and there is no subsequent written agreement between the finder and the corporation; the finder, if his information contributed to the merger or acquisition, generally is entitled to a fee.

Nevertheless, there have been and will continue to be disputes over such fees, both with established business-consulting firms as well as those often described as "bucket shop" or "fly-by-night" operators. The latter are characterized by a technique that consists of sending letters to executives of corporations suggesting a particular company as a target for takeover. If the corporation eventually does acquire the target company, the broker will present himself and demand a fee for services rendered. The corporation may find itself in the position of having to pay such a fee when in fact it did not use the information because, say, the information was sent to an executive who promptly disposed of it. Such disputes are extremely sensitive matters. Their sensitivity arises from several factors. The size of the fee, in the case of a major acquisition, can be quite large. To defend the case, the corporation may have to make public its merger strategy and the sources of its merger advice. Also, the corporation may have to prove a negative—that it did not use the information it actually received.

A corporation actively involved in acquisitions or mergers should prepare a written policy concerning finder's fees. Such a policy should deal both with the retention of these business brokers and the handling of unsolicited pieces of information. In particular, the policy should attempt to assist its users in identifying exactly when a person is acting as a merger or business broker in order to protect the corporation from future liability. Although the policy cannot stop unsolicited proposals from being made, it can establish procedures that can minimize their impact; further, it can limit who retains legitimate brokers.

These procedures should require that all unsolicited proposals be forwarded to a central location. If the recipient can identify a mailing as a potential proposal (by the return address, for example), it should be forwarded to the central location unopened. Otherwise it should be read only enough to identify the subject matter and forwarded on. No copies should be made along the way; only records of its transmittal should be kept. The person to whom it is sent should not be one with responsibilities in the merger and acquisition area, so there can be no question of his or her misuse merely by reading it. The entire proposal should be returned to the sender by registered mail, return receipt requested, with a cover letter noting it is unsolicited and no copy has been made. No copy should be kept of the proposal, only the cover letter, which should not make reference to the contents of the proposal. If desired, the corporation can advise the sender how to formally submit a proposal.

## Outside Independent Public Accountants

Corporations increasingly have written policies concerning their relations with their outside independent public accountants. Due to changes in the responsibilities of such accountants in recent years, some major accounting firms prefer that all contacts with them be made by one corporate officer. Generally they are concerned about non-audit services in addition to those requested by the board of directors for reports to the Securities and Exchange Commission (SEC), stock exchanges, and shareholders. This is a consulting-related issue, for the major accounting firms often provide business- and personnel-consulting services. Such a request could be for the branch of the accounting firm to audit the financial status of a subsidiary being dissolved or to establish cash-management procedures in a particular subsidiary. These requests could constitute a conflict for the main accounting firm, which then would have to audit its own audit or evaluate the efficiency and security of procedures that it developed.

To avoid these potential conflicts, the corporation should establish internal procedures identifying its independent auditors, either prohibiting their use for any other purpose or requiring that all requests for their use be processed through one corporate officer. This officer could be the one with whom the accounting firm works most frequently, the officer who prepares the corporation's report to the SEC, or both. The latter officer, usually the general counsel or corporate secretary, at least should be aware of the use of the outside independent public accountants. The SEC requires that firms operating as independent auditors must disclose the nature and extent of nonaudit services provided to their client corporations, so that the shareholders and the public can evaluate if the independence of the auditors has been compromised.

## Outside Legal Counsel and Lobbyists

Although not arising as frequently as the question of the employment of the independent auditors, some review should be made of any policies regarding the retention of outside legal counsel. Outside legal counsel may serve in a quasi-consulting relationship to a corporation. If lawyers are being hired just to provide advice and not appear in court or before a judicial agency, they are serving in a consulting relationship. The advice rendered by lawyers that may put them in a consulting relationship includes the following:

Designing employee benefit packages, a service also performed by accounting and actuarial firms

Advising on merger and acquisitions, a service also performed by merger consultants and investment bankers

Reviewing consumer complaint or employee grievance systems, a service also performed by communications consultants

If there is no adequate outside legal counsel policy, lawyers should be subject to the controls and standards in the policies set forth earlier in this chapter and in the sample policy.

Occasionally, outside attorneys in turn hire specialist attorneys to provide unusual or very narrow advice to the law firm. This often happens in areas that traditionally have been legal specialities, such as admiralty or patent law. In these cases, the firm's own lawyers are hiring consultants, and corporations retaining outside counsel should be aware of this for several reasons:

The lawyers are hiring another person who also may deem himself to represent the corporation and thereby expose the corporation to additional liability

The corporation should be aware that the lawyers it has hired do not have the needed expertise and must seek outside aid

The corporation may wish to exercise direct control over the legal (and, by implication, other) consultants its own lawyers hire and whom it ultimately must pay

The corporation may find that its reputation is affected by association with these consultants and thus should exercise some say in their initial and ultimate utilization

Some lawyers are lobbyists, but not all lobbyists are lawyers. The use of lobbyists is particularly sensitive, as they are consultants, and all of the controls and contractual issues surrounding the retention and use of outside consultants apply to them. In addition, lobbyists represent the corporation in the political arena. The power to retain them should be limited to a small number of senior executives, and they should be subject to continual supervision. The areas of particular supervision should include:

prompt registration of all lobbyists working on behalf of the corporation, if required (some state and federal laws require both the lobbyist and the retaining corporation to register if legislative lobbying is being conducted)

careful review of all lobbyist expenditures (lobbyists often have been viewed as conduits for "payoffs" to public officials, either directly or through excessive spending or entertaining)

the exact nature of the relationship, if any, between a corporation's political action committee and its lobbyists

## Risk Management

The increasingly important area of risk management includes not only the purchase of insurance but loss control and management of claims, as well as the analysis of risks. Corporations who have adopted or will adopt formal written policies on corporate risk management should remember that the retention of consultants is a matter appropriate for review by a risk-management officer. The risk-management officer may wish to verify that all insurance issues raised in the consulting agreement are resolved. Some examples of those are retaining "key man" insurance on a consultant whose project is critical to the corporation or requiring the consultant to show proof of any coverage (such as worker's compensation insurance) that the consultant legally is required to have. How the review is conducted is a matter for the risk-management officer to determine, but once written policies are adopted, they should cover the retention of outside consultants.

## Insider Trading

Due to the restrictions imposed by the federal and state securities legislation, most corporations with publicly listed stock have adopted formal written policies dealing with transactions in their own stocks and bonds. These are designed to cover the improper use of inside information by all employees as well as all pur-chases and sales by officers and directors who are not acting on inside infor-mation. Although the current scope of securities laws, as interpreted by the SEC and the federal courts, does not include consultants as insiders subject to the requirements and penalties of the federal securities law, corporations with pub-licly traded securities will do well to think about this issue. In particular, it may be desirable to require that consultants be made aware of the corporation's pol-icies on sales of its own securities. A statement that the consultants are aware of the policies, as suggested in the sample policy language, may be of assis-tance. It also may be advisable to require that the corporate policy limiting sales based upon inside knowledge apply not only to employees and their families but also to individuals serving in a consulting relationship with the corporation.

## Foreign Corrupt Practices Act

A related policy about which much has been written is that required by the For-eign Corrupt Practices Act. This act governs the payments overseas made to secure preferential government or customer actions. The literature on the act and its effects is massive. As a result of the act, corporations have had to establish procedures in order to assure compliance with it and other federal laws. Many of the publicized cases leading to passage of the act involved so-called consultants; the corporation creating or revising a policy because of the act should be aware that improper actions of consultants could expose it to prosecution. Corporate policy should include specific limitations on the retention of overseas consultants, how they are paid, their specific authority, who may hire them and when they can be used. This policy should be discussed with consultants who should then agree, in writing, to be bound by this policy (and any other ethical or business practice corporate policies). Only with the use of specific policies and effective ongoing monitoring can a corporation protect itself from liability.

## References

The number of state laws dealing with employee records and references is increasing rapidly. These laws will require most corporations to have written guidelines dealing with the retention of employee records and the giving of ref-erences on former or current employees to third parties. In formulating such pol-icies, a corporation should consider whether it should provide references on consultants, both individual and corporate, that it has retained in the past. Today, the statutory definitions of employees do not include consultants; these definitions are not uniform, however, and it is possible that in the future a consultant may do such sensitive or supervisory tasks that he or she may be deemed an employee, at least for the purposes of these laws.

### Conflicts of Interest

Another policy should cover possible conflicts of interest. A corporation should consider asking consultants whether they are currently working for other businesses, which could place the consultant in a conflict of interest. A useful standard to apply is the same standard applied to employees—that is, whether the other business is in a directly competitive situation. The issue also can be handled in the agreement with the consultant. The form discussed in chapter 7 provides sample language governing corporate opportunities and conflicts of interest.

### SAMPLE CORPORATE POLICY—PREPARATION OF PROCEDURES

Although every corporation differs in its approach to corporate policies, each should consider preparing corporate policies on the use and retention of outside consultants. This section reviews a decentralized or directional policy, included in the Appendix. A decentralized policy requires each division to prepare its own procedures and guidelines concerning the retention of outside consultants, based upon a broad directive in the policy. This approach is particularly useful in an organization where each division of the corporation has different needs for consultants, for example, engineering consultants in one division, marketing consultants for another, and compensation specialists for a third. The guidelines in paragraph 1 of the policy statement are designed to reflect this. A smaller or more centralized corporation may wish to adopt paragraph 1 as a directive without more detailed procedures.

Regardless of the size of the corporation, the retention and use of consultants should be subject to both budget and contract review, at least for agreements for services in excess of a fixed amount. This assures the corporation that its procedures are being followed, particularly that the terms of the consulting agreement, the description of the services to be rendered, and the total compensation are defined clearly in advance. In addition, legal review should be required for all consulting relationships covering services performed for longer than a period of one year, due to the statute of frauds (discussed in chapter 5). During the legal review, the corporation can require that negotiations with the consultant be based upon its own form of agreement or can focus the negotiations on a contract clause of particular importance to it. Paragraph 1 is designed to assure that such review is obtained:

1. Each Division issues procedures, to be approved by _____, which require that:
   a. every requirement for outside consultants be justified in writing;
   b. agreements with outside consultants be complete and specify a fixed period of performance for the services to be provided; and
   c. legal and budget review of all agreements for services in excess of one year or costing over $5,000.00 be obtained.

## Coverage

The first problem in establishing a corporate policy on the hiring of outside consultants is to specify exactly what outside consultants are. This is related directly to the kind of control the corporation wishes to exercise over the use of consultants. In the sample corporate policy, the definition of outside consultants is one generally accepted, but as with all such definitions it includes certain policy judgments within it.

*Definition:* Outside consultants provide those personal and professional services of a purely advisory nature, such as the development of policy. They do not perform operating functions or supervise those functions. Outside consultants' services include advice about management and administration; these services do not include commercial and industrial services or research. The services of outside consultants are provided by persons and firms generally considered to have expertise, knowledge, and ability of particular value to a Division.

By defining a consultant as one who does not perform or supervise operating functions, a corporation bars any outside consultant from carrying out such duties. It is not improbable that a consultant may be hired, in part, to supervise operating functions, a fact about which the federal government is particularly sensitive. In addition, some consultants perform what may be described as research services on a contract basis. If a corporation believes it will be retaining consultants for such services, it should include them in the definition and thus in the policy's coverage. If a function is not included in the definition, then a consultant may be hired but not be subject to the restrictions of this policy. For example, if the policy requires prior approval to hire consultants, but the definition of consulting excludes research services, a consultant doing research could be hired without prior approval.

### Limitations on the Use of Consultants

Paragraph 2 of the policy attempts to limit those situations where outside consultants may be used.

2.  Outside consultants may be used by Divisions when:
    a. specialized opinions or professional or technical advice is required and is not available within the Corporation;

    b. an outside point of view on a critical issue is necessary;

    c. state-of-the-art knowledge, education, or research is needed;

    d. opinion(s) of noted experts with national or international prestige is essential to the success of a key project; or

    e. services of special personnel who are not needed full time or cannot serve full time are required.

Again these definitions are general but permit management to control the use of consultants. In light of the comments prohibiting outside consultants from making management decisions or bypassing or undermining personnel limits, more detailed requirements may be counterproductive. Of course, as difficult situations arise from time to time, such guidelines can be modified. More specific guidelines can be developed by reference to the current U.S. Office of Management and Budget policy on consultants, included in the Appendix.

The origin of the federal policy should be kept in mind before deciding to adopt it without substantial change. The federal government is the largest consumer of consulting services in the nation. There are no official estimates, but unofficial estimates indicate more than $33 billion is spent each year for various kinds of consulting services. The lack of control in the retention and use of consultants by the government has led to hearings by congressional committees, investigations by the General Accounting Office, and numerous legislative proposals. In response to this, the Office of Management and Budget developed its guidelines to accomplish several goals, which included:

To establish reasonably uniform definitions of consulting services for record-keeping purposes

To collect information on the total expenditures for consulting services

To control the excessive use of consultants by federal agencies for both political and budgetary reasons

## Prior Approval

Paragraph 3 of the policy statement is designed to assure that operating managers cannot retain consultants without approval from at least one senior layer of management.

3. Each Division establishes specific levels of delegations of authority to approve the use of outside consultants. At least _____ levels of approval are required to hire an outside consultant.

Requiring prior approval can accomplish several goals:

It can force managers to articulate more completely the reason for using consultants and for selecting a particular consultant

It permits review of the decision to hire a consultant to determine if the terms of retention are consistent with the corporation's budget and legal policies

It allows senior management to suggest consideration of alternative consultants or of alternative methods of accomplishing the same result, including the use of other consultants already working for the corporation

A corporation, of course, may require that only one particular person or one particular office be empowered to retain consultants or that such an office must review the retention of consultants where the contract will involve more than a predetermined amount of money.

## Optional Provisions

The pages following the first sample policy set forth additional optional policy provisions dealing with outside consultants. They can be included within the basic policy and are designed to meet particular needs of the small, medium, and large company.

"MOTHERHOOD" STATEMENT
The first optional provision requires a consultant to be bound by the corporation's policies.

1. Any outside consultant must agree, in writing, to be bound by the corporation's policies.

This may sound like a "motherhood" statement, but it is of particular importance. As was discussed earlier, the use of consultants in certain overseas situations can give rise to serious problems in complying with the Foreign Corrupt Practices Act. By requiring a consultant to be bound by corporate policies, the corporation at least can assure itself that the consultant understands the scope of the corporation's position on business ethics and conflict of interest. In addition, it enables the corporation to subject a consultant to a wide variety of administrative policies, such as restrictions on travel expenditures, without having to repeat them in the consultant policy or in the consulting agreement. The corporation should be sure that it wants the consultant bound by all of the corporation's policies; if there is some doubt about this, then which policies are binding must be spelled out.

Of course, to be bound, the consultant must be given a copy of the policies. Here, too, management should review the policies to decide if an outside consultant should get copies of all the corporation's policies.

FINAL REPORT
The second optional clause requires that a copy of the final report of each consultant, or summary of its services, be sent to a particular administrative officer upon completion of the assignment.

2. A copy of the final report of each outside consultant, or a summary of the services performed if no final report is prepared, will be forwarded to _____ upon completion of the assignment.

This is designed to collect in one place the information and services provided by the consultants, a particularly critical matter in highly decentralized corporations. It is not impossible to imagine a circumstance in which one unit of a corporation asks for certain kinds of market research services to be performed, and later that year, another unit of that corporation requires similar services to be performed by another consultant elsewhere in the country. These reports, in addition to preventing duplication in hiring, provide a library available for executive review. By referring to these libraries, executives and managers can have a better understanding of precisely how to frame the assignment given to a consultant and a standard against which to review the quality of the final product. This in turn can be significant if the contract with a consultant requires—which it should—that the final work product be acceptable to the corporation. Referring to analogous reports by competing consultants may give a corporation a strong legal basis upon which to reject a report as inadequate if the corporation has retained that right.

### APPRAISAL AND REVIEW

The third optional paragraph requires that the executive in charge of the assignment prepare a consultant appraisal and review form to be forwarded to a senior administrative officer. A suggested form is included in the Appendix. This clause, together with optional paragraph 4(b), permits the corporation to ascertain whether consultants under consideration are competent and whether they have performed in an acceptable manner on other assignments. Paragraph 5, which requires a consultant retention form to be completed, when used in conjunction with paragraph 4, permits central control of consultants to assure that there is no duplication in their retention. It also permits the corporation to control potential conflicts of interest, a matter that should be of concern to both the consultant and the corporation.

3. The Executive in charge of the assignment will prepare a Consultant Appraisal and Review Form at the conclusion of an assignment and forward it to _____.
4. (b.) obtain from _____ an appraisal of the consultant under

consideration and recommendations of other firms capable of carrying out the assignment, based upon a corporate appraisal previously submitted, internal recommendations, outside references, interviews, and other searches for competent consultants not previously used by the corporation.

5. Upon retaining an outside consultant, the Executive in charge of the assignment will complete a Consultant Retention Form and forward it to _____.

SIMILAR WORK CLAUSE

Paragraph 4(a) is designed to provide an additional benefit to the corporation. It requires the executive seeking to retain a consultant to ascertain that another part of the corporation is not having similar work done now or in the past. If similar work is under way, management may wish to consider approaching the consultant already under contract to determine if he can perform the related duties efficiently and without interfering with his current work.

4. Prior to retaining any outside consultant, the Executive in charge of the assignment will:
   a. ascertain that the same or substantially similar work has not been done or is not now being done elsewhere in the corporation by contacting _____;

If similar work has been performed, management should review that past performance. Management may find that the new project has been done either partly or entirely. Even if this is not the case, management may review past work and reports to learn from them. It can learn how to specify the services it wants, how to supervise such a project, or how to select a consultant for the current project. Management may even find that the consultant who worked for the corporation before should be considered for this project.

BUDGET CLAUSE

Optional paragraph 6 is a budgetary clause that can appear either in a policy on consultants or in a separate budget manual.

6. Each Division, in its annual budget, must include a detailed description of the nature and projected cost of any consulting work being requested as well as the names of the consultants being considered.

Use of this clause, which requires a detailed description of projected consulting to be included in the budget as well as the names of consultants under consideration, is designed to control nonapproved consulting, particularly when used with optional paragraph 7.

7. Any outside consulting needed after the annual budget has been approved and not detailed in that budget must be approved by _____ if the estimated annual cost of the contract will exceed $_____.

Paragraph 6 also assures that corporate management can exercise central review over the total cost of consultants to determine if it is preferable to have such work completely internalized, either now or in the future. In addition, by setting forth the names of consultants under consideration, it permits management to utilize its assessment of the prior performance of consultants in other areas to make more effective use of the consultants. Chapter 3 contains additional budgetary guidance.

## CONSULTANT RETENTION FORM

The consultant retention form is self-explanatory. The form requires that the consulting firm be retained in writing either by a letter or a contract and that the contract accompany this form. The subject of contracts is dealt with in more detail in chapters 6 and 7. Many simple consulting relationships do not require major complex contracts, although all of the issues raised in chapter 5 should be considered before any consulting relationship is created. In those cases where a consultant is being retained for less than one year to do a specific assignment not involving substantial expenses to the employer, a letter agreement may suffice. Letter agreements are discussed in more detail in chapter 6.

## CONSULTANT RETENTION FORM

Name and address of consulting firm retained:

_____

_____

Member of firm responsible for this account: _____

Date retained: _____ Retention authorized by: _____

Nature of assignment:

(  ) Planning         (  ) Employee         (  ) Taxes
(  ) Marketing             relations         (  ) Organizational
(  ) Regulatory        (  ) Investments     (  ) Financial
(  ) Customer        (  ) Real estate       (  ) Acquisitions
     relations         (  ) Government
                    relations

(  ) Other _____

Brief summary of assignment: _____

_____

The consulting firm retained has been given a contract confirming its retention and specifying the terms and conditions of its assignment. A copy of it is attached.

## SAMPLE LETTER CONFIRMING RETENTION OF A CONSULTANT

The sample letter confirming retention of a consultant assumes that the executive in charge of the consulting assignment at the corporation has discussed the terms and conditions of the consultant's retention and that these terms are acceptable. It puts in writing the conversation between the parties and indicates clearly that the executive at the corporation is in charge of the project. In particular, this executive will control access to confidential information and resolve any conflicts that the consultant may have regarding the scope of the assignment or corporate personnel. This letter is not a contract and should not be used instead of a contract.

## SAMPLE LETTER CONFIRMING
## RETENTION OF A CONSULTANT

(Addressee)

Dear Sir/Madam:

We are pleased that you will be able to work with us in connection with the _____ project.

As we have discussed, I will be involved in this project and will resolve those major issues arising during this project that involve either policy considerations or strategy. If you have any questions regarding which tasks you are to perform or how you are to perform them, I will answer them. In addition, if there are any questions on the manner in which you are to proceed, such as access to confidential company information, I will be responsible for resolving them.

I am enclosing a copy of the agreement we have previously discussed, setting forth the terms and conditions of your assignment. Please sign one copy and return it to me. Keep the other for your files.

I have enclosed a copy of our billing procedures, which you will need. Please see that all services performed for us and all statements rendered in connection with those services are prepared in conformance with these procedures.

We look forward to working with you.

Very truly yours,

(signed by the Executive
in charge of the assignment)

## CONSULTANT BILLING PROCEDURE

Accompanying the retention letter should be a billing procedure. If the corporation does not have billing procedures, it should consider adopting the billing form in the Appendix. This form stipulates that the firm retained has a standard daily or hourly rate, which will be used in this case. In addition, it clearly notes that any other persons outside the consulting company may be used on this project only after they have been retained by the corporation and not by the consultant.

Except where otherwise agreed to in writing, the Corporation is to be charged for services rendered on its behalf only on the basis of the application of the Firm's standard hourly or daily rate for the categories of employees performing the services. In addition, the Corporation will be charged for services rendered by other consultants, accountants, or experts only when they have been retained directly by the Corporation's Executive in charge of the assignment.

The billing procedures then outline the billing statements and the cycle upon which they should be submitted. They provide that the consultant is not required to submit bills for nominal amounts but that he should submit large bills every thirty days. To exercise special financial control, the consultant is required to submit a bill every calendar quarter, even if he has not done so beforehand. The problem of year-end bills paid within the tax year is covered by a sentence requiring that statements for the period through November 30 must be submitted by December 10. Finally, to deal with the estimated year-end obligations of the corporate unit in question, the policy requires that the December work be estimated and submitted at the beginning of January.

A statement for services rendered may be submitted to the Corporation as frequently as the consultant desires. In any case, a statement must be submitted to the Corporation within 30 days following the end of any month in which the total services and disbursements exceed _____, and within 30 days following the end of the calendar quarter. For accounting purposes, a statement through November 30 must be submitted by December 10. A written estimate of the total December statement must be submitted on the first working day each January.

The billing procedures set forth the items the bill should cover, enabling the hiring corporation to evaluate the quantity of time spent on the project as well as the level and number of employees involved.

1. The number of hours or days spent by each category of employee of the Firm on the assignment;

2. The billing rate for each category of employee of the Firm on the assignment;
3. The total disbursements made to other consultants, accountants, and experts;
4. All expenses and disbursements;
5. The total due the Firm for the billing period.

In addition, the statement shall indicate by whom it was prepared and the period it covers and shall be accompanied by any statements rendered the Firm by other consultants, accountants, and experts.

It is particularly important that management have a general idea whether the work requires high-, medium-, or low-level personnel; management should be able to determine this from these billings.

The billing procedures also require that the consultant's statement detail the services performed during the period covered by the statement.

Although it is assumed that the Corporation Executive in charge of this assignment is fully familiar with the nature of the services performed by the consultant on each assignment during the period covered by the statement, the statement should detail the various services that were performed in connection with the assignment.

This is designed to serve several purposes. First, it operates as a control on the consultant to assure that accurate records are being kept of the services being performed and for which the corporation is being billed. This is critical, as many of the services being performed may be off site and without the prior approval of the corporation. Second, it enables the corporation to determine early on whether the consulting firm is heading in a wrong direction on the project. For example, if a marketing project involves a question of retailing goods through discount stores, statements that outline meetings with wholesalers or surveys of factories should be questioned to assure that the individuals working on the project understand the limited nature of their assignment. Third, it enables corporate management to evaluate the work of the consulting organization as a whole, as well as that of individual consultants. This can be of particular assistance in completing the consultant appraisal and review form, as it permits the appraisal of an organization and of individuals who later may be a part of another consulting organization.

## CONSULTANT APPRAISAL AND REVIEW FORM

One way to evaluate consultant services is to use an appraisal and review form. The form in the Appendix is designed to be filled in after a consulting company has finished its project. Optional policy paragraphs 3 and 4 require management to complete them and refer to them before hiring a consultant. The appraisal and review form is keyed to the retention form, but the retention form does not have to be completed for a corporation to use an appraisal form. The retention form is designed for prospective administrative control; the appraisal serves other purposes.

In the appraisal form, the executive reviews and evaluates several different aspects of the consulting services performed. First, the executive evaluates the services of the member of the consulting firm responsible for the account. These services include such matters as supervision, consultation with the client, control over expenditures, and final presentation. The executive in charge also evaluates other members of the consulting firm principally involved on the assignment; this typically includes junior partners in the firm or senior- and middle-line analysts. The purpose of this is to assist the corporation in future relations with both this and other firms. For example, if the corporate executive felt the work product was good but that the partner in charge of the account at the consulting firm did not exercise strong budgetary constraint, he or she could recommend that the firm be used in the same area but that a different partner be in charge of the account. Similarly, if one or more of the consulting firm's employees are highly regarded by the employing corporation, special note should be made of this, as the consulting industry, as in so many other service industries, often sees aspiring individuals leaving major consulting firms to join smaller consulting firms or to establish their own businesses. By evaluating key consultants, the corporation is able to follow a particularly competent individual to his or her next place of employment and retain that person there.

Finally, the executive in charge is asked to evaluate the overall quality of the service provided by the consulting firm on this assignment, a matter that includes all prior appraisals.

In evaluating the performance of the consultant, the executive must keep in mind the nature of the assignment given to the consultant, the working relationship established with the consultant, and the results anticipated at the beginning of the assignment. The evaluation should consider at least the following issues:

Whether the consultant accomplished the goals set out at the beginning, or as modified during the project

Whether changes were made in the nature of assignment and why. For example, did the corporation fail to define the task or was the consultant unable to perform as promised or desired?

Whether the corporation's personnel gained from working with the consultant. Was this intended or not? How beneficial was the exposure? Could that benefit have been acquired elsewhere at a lower cost?

How was the final work product delivered to the corporation? Was it clear and immediately useable or did it have to be explained?

Whether the solutions, if any, proposed by the Consultant were responsive to the problems identified at the beginning, whether they are practical, and whether they will be implemented. If they are not being implemented, why not?

Whether the project was completed or not. Was it finished on time?

Was the cost of the project within the original contract limit or within initial cost estimates? Why was there a difference? Are the results of the project beneficial in relation to the project's estimated and final costs?

Did the project leave issues unresolved or deferred for further consideration pending implementation of the study? Why?

In preparing the evaluation, absolute candor is required. The corporation must acknowledge where its actions caused problems. For example, the final cost of a project may be higher than anticipated, but the reason may be the corporation's failure to coöperate promptly with the consultant. Just as the success of a project is credited to all parties, the failure of a project may be the fault of all concerned. The corporation must have a good consultant, and the consultant must have a good client.

The executive then is asked specifically to recommend whether the services of this consulting firm should be used for more work in particular areas, should be limited to work only in certain areas, or should not be used at all on any future assignments. These evaluations are quite important and should be kept confidential. In addition to making other comments, a corporation may request that a copy of the final report, if it is not too long or technical, be included with the appraisal form, so that individuals considering the use of this consulting firm in the future may have a chance to review the major part of the work product.

Included in the Appendix is an appraisal form based on one developed by the U.S. Department of Health and Human Services. This form is designed to exercise budgetary control by forcing those who purchased consulting services to show that the consultant complied with the contract. It is not designed to evaluate a consultant's performance to determine if that consultant should be considered for a future contract.

## ALTERNATIVE SAMPLE CORPORATE POLICY

An alternative form of policy sets forth direct procedures governing the mechanics of retaining, paying, and evaluating outside consultants. Such a policy is included in the Appendix and keyed to the retention form, billing procedures, statement, sample letter, and appraisal and review form. In contrast to the first, this policy does not set forth when or under what conditions a consultant may be retained; rather, it establishes who may retain him and the mechanical processes governing the retention and payment of consultants. The centralized policy is useful in an organization which has a centralized budget and financial control system, which is small enough that all retention decisions can be made efficiently by one person or office, or one which seeks to limit the use (or overuse) of consultants through central control. This policy could also be adopted by an operating division to supplement the broad, decentralized policy described earlier in this chapter. In particular, these procedures could be a model for those required by paragraphs 1 and 3 of the broader statement.

# CHAPTER FIVE

# Legal Issues

## WHY LEGAL ISSUES ARE INVOLVED IN THE CONSULTING RELATIONSHIP

The consulting agreement must cover the elements found in the traditional employment contract as well as some "independent contractor" elements appropriate to this hybrid relationship. The topics to be included in any consulting agreement are only a core list. Consideration of management questions (raised in chapter 3) will indicate additional topics for inclusion. As the following chapters will show, in preparing a complete and complex contract or a simple letter agreement, additional topics also will emerge for consideration. Consideration of all topics will provide for a complete working legal document.

## SOME BROAD TOPICS THAT SHOULD BE CONSIDERED IN DRAFTING CONSULTING AGREEMENTS

In light of the special nature of the consulting relationship, the following broad topics should be considered in drafting every consulting agreement.

1. Services to be performed
2. Independent contractor status; work product; copyrights and patents
3. Compensation; costs
4. Duration
5. Termination
6. Modification; nonassignability
7. Restrictive covenants
8. Applicable law
9. Manner of giving notice

As mentioned earlier, to avoid the problems of the statute of frauds, every consulting agreement should be in writing.

### Services to Be Performed

Throughout this section, the parties will be called "the Corporation" and "the Consultant." In drafting an agreement, the Corporation should not be called "the

Employer," as use of this term could undermine the independent contractor status of the consultant.

One of the most common, troublesome problems in the consulting relationship is the failure to define clearly the work to be performed. One method of defining the scope of the task is to have the consultant prepare a written proposal, which then can be modified in negotiations and incorporated into the final agreement. Where appropriate, efforts should be made to cover such matters as regular work reports and, if possible, to specify the expected result of the consultant's performance. The corporation may wish to specify also that it will do business only with a partner or principal of the consulting firm. Although the consultant has an implied legal obligation to do the work diligently and in a reasonably skillful way, the corporation is well advised to set standards of performance.

The obligations of the consultant to serve and the corporation to pay must not be illusory ones, or the agreement will not be a valid, enforceable contract. A promise by the corporation to employ the consultant as long as it suits the corporation is regarded as an illusory promise and cannot be enforced. An agreement providing that the consultant will perform all services of a certain described nature that the corporation decides need doing is not illusory.

Some businesses feel that loose contracting practices in a consulting agreement are desirable because they allow room for both sides to maneuver. Experience has shown that the possibilities of unenforceability and future disputes over the scope of the work represent major risks. A clear, detailed statement of the work to be performed is absolutely indispensible to a valid, enforceable agreement. Any looseness in specifications should be intentional and adopted in full recognition of the business and legal risks involved.

In an agreement where the consultant promises to provide services "as required and as the corporation may direct," the consultant's duty to perform is, by implication, conditional upon receiving a notice of instructions and being given a reasonable time to provide the services. Implications should be avoided; precise language should be used.

If the agreement makes no provision for the time of performance and the parties ultimately must go to court over this question, a court is free to fix a "reasonable" time for performance. If the agreement defines the time even incompletely or imperfectly, however, a court will not be free to attach its own conception of what is a reasonable time for performance but will be bound by the agreement. The agreement therefore should define the time of performance if it is important either to the consultant or to the corporation. The definition of performance should be done with great care and specificity.

### Independent Contractor Status; Work Product; Copyrights and Patents

As discussed earlier, the status of an independent contractor is a key element in creating the consulting relationship. For this reason, it must be dealt with in the agreement. Merely stating in an agreement that the consultant's relationship to the corporation is that of an independent contractor does not create that relationship automatically. Such a statement is, however, a good starting place.

When a corporation gives up the right to direct and control the consultant and the consultant's employees regarding the result to be accomplished and the manner and means by which that result is obtained, an independent contractor relationship is created. The corporation always must respect this allocation of control, as it is not only the contract's language but also the actual practice of the parties that determines their true relationship. If the corporation exercises direct control over the consultant and the consultant's employees, it may subject the corporation to liability for the torts of the consultant and its employees.

The agreement should cover not only the ownership and disposition of any patentable or copyrightable work product but also should set forth the corporation's right to obtain the consultant's work product during the term of the agreement or at its termination, whether or not patentable or copyrightable. The corporation also may wish to provide for indemnification by the consultant for patent and/or copyright infringement. The importance of these types of clauses may be understood by reference to a federal contracting problem reported by the *Washington Post*. To entice bidders, a federal agency seeking an outside evaluation of an experimental drug agreed that the consultant testing the drug would be able to exploit the drug commercially at the end of the contract. The contract provided that the consultant could keep the treatment records and use them in seeking approval from the Food and Drug Administration to sell the drug. The agency then decided to terminate the project before it was completed. The agency found that it was not entitled to any of the treatment records from the consultant, even though the consultant no longer could hope to market the drug. In essence, the agency paid for research it will never get and no one will ever use.

## Compensation; Costs

Compensation under a consulting agreement is an area of potential controversy, particularly when it is open-ended. Where open-ended pricing is the only feasible approach, the consultant should be required to let the corporation know when a predetermined threshold figure is imminent so that the corporation can control its financial exposure. If the contract pays costs plus a fixed fee, there should be a defined maximum on the total costs. Further, if the agreement permits the consultant to pass on increases in its own personnel costs, the consultant should give prior notice of these new costs and the agreement should provide specifically when such increases will be reimbursed under the agreement.

When a consulting agreement provides for payment of a flat fee upon the completion of a task, both sides must consider what compensation, if any, the consultant should receive if full performance becomes impossible. If the agreement is with an individual consultant, the law appears to be that the consultant is entitled to the fair value of any services rendered for which, because illness or death prevented completing his performance, he could not recover unless the agreement clearly makes the whole performance a prerequisite to payment for any part of the work. When outside events of other kinds, such as a supervening law or the conduct of a third person on whose coöperation the ability to perform depends, make complete performance impossible, payment should be provided to the extent of the fair value of partial performance rendered while performance was still possible.

## Duration

Any unwritten agreement that cannot be performed within one year may run afoul of the statute of frauds. Thus any consulting relationship should be created in writing for a stated term. In drafting a duration clause, specificity is again necessary, as an agreement stating that the contract is to last "so long as conditions warrant" may be too indefinite for enforcement.

Further, the manner in which the term is stated can have varying consequences. For example, if the consultant has an agreement with option periods exercisable by him and is discharged wrongfully, the corporation may be liable for the present value of the unexpired term of the agreement plus all option periods. A contract renewable at the corporation's option or by mutual agreement therefore is preferable to one renewable at the consultant's option.

If the corporation has no use for the consultant's work after a certain date, the corporation should insist that it be released from the contract if the consultant's performance has not been rendered satisfactorily by that time.

## Termination

It is not unusual for a commercial contract to state that it can be terminated for "good cause shown." Using such a term invites lawsuits, however, since the existence of "good cause" may be a question of fact that can put a case directly to a jury. The grounds for termination should, where possible, be categorized or defined fully.

Some agreements include an "option to cancel." The power created by this provision is not generally made conditional upon the corporation's dissatisfaction with the results; it is a power to cancel if and when the corporation desires. Such a power does not mean the contract is illusory. No action for breach of contract can be maintained against the corporation if it has exercised this power to cancel in accord with its terms and otherwise has complied with the contract. Making an analogy to the law of employment contracts, when an agreement provides that the consultant's performance must be to the corporation's satisfaction, a court will not inquire into the reason for the termination under this clause so long as it is made in good faith. That is, the corporation must in fact be dissatisfied; its dissatisfaction does not have to be reasonable.

A clause providing for automatic termination upon the occurrence of a specified event generally is to be regarded as giving either party an option to terminate the agreement by giving notice to the other party of the event. Upon receipt of that notice, the contract is terminated.

## Restrictive Covenants

Although an employee, and thus a consultant, has an implied legal duty to refrain from deceiving the corporation, from entering into relations giving him an interest inconsistent with that of the corporation, and from disclosing or using to his own advantage secret information confidentially entrusted to him, the consulting agreement should deal specifically with the problems of confidentiality of trade secrets, conflicts of interest, and noncompetitive covenants. A noncompetitive covenant is a promise that the consultant will not work for a direct competitor of the corporation for a limited amount of time, say one year, after the contract with the corporation has expired.

In general, noncompetitive covenants are valid and enforceable in court either by money damages or by injunctions. Although such clauses are vulnerable to attack if they are too restrictive, the fact that the consulting agreement is not an employer-employee contract may give the consulting parties greater freedom to impose restrictions and restraints than would be the case otherwise.

## Modification; Nonassignability

The relationship between the consultant and the corporation can become quite informal, especially in agreements where the duties of the consultant are somewhat open-ended. Care must be taken that all potential modifications of the agreement, including instructions, are in writing. Oral modifications and instructions can cause problems with the statute of frauds and the necessary specificity of the consultant's duties.

The decision to make the agreement nonassignable is particularly important. For example, in a cost-plus agreement, the compensation paid to any subcontractor may become a reimburseable cost, in addition to the consultant's fee, potentially increasing the total amount the corporation may have to pay. When the consultant is employed because of his unique areas of expertise, by making his performance nondelegable the agreement may become one for personal services. As discussed in chapter 8, agreements that are regarded as personal service contracts are difficult to enforce by a suit or an injunction. On the other hand, permitting the consultant to assign part or all of his performance could negate any clause stating that the corporation will deal only with the principals or partners of the consulting firm.

## Applicable Law

In employment agreements, establishing which law applies is important when the employee will work in a state or country other than his own, due to the question of the applicability of worker's compensation statutes. In any consulting agreement with an individual, applicable law should be covered in case the agreement is later characterized as an employment contract.

In general, stating the law applicable to a consulting agreement is important, as by its terms the contract may not specify where it is to be performed. Usually, the place where a contract is to be performed determines which law applies. If this is not known, the parties cannot know which law a court will apply in a dispute. It is generally accepted that an agreement concerning applicable law will be respected and enforced by the courts, providing the law specified has some reasonable or foreseeable connection with the transaction at its beginning.

## Manner of Giving Notice

The notice required for termination should be discussed in the agreement. If the agreement is not for a fixed term and thus able to be terminated at will, there is no general legal principle that requires notice of a specified length of time. As was indicated earlier, all notices and instructions, should be in writing. The agreement should provide how notice is given, to whom it is given, and how much in advance it must be given.

# CHAPTER SIX

# The Letter Agreement

## THE DIFFERENCE BETWEEN A LETTER AGREEMENT AND A CONSULTING CONTRACT

Not all consulting agreements have to be complicated. The long-term consulting agreement should cover a large number of specific issues; by the very nature of the amount of money involved and the scope of the service to be provided, a lengthy and complicated agreement may be necessary. In many cases, however, a shorter and more standardized agreement may be appropriate. This kind of agreement is called the letter agreement.

Management control over such letter agreements can be accomplished in a number of ways. The letter agreement may have to be executed by individuals in the corporation of a certain rank or higher. If the corporation uses consultants for a variety of small projects on a frequent basis, budgetary controls may be sufficient to deal with excessive use of consultants. In this situation, the letter agreement may be used freely. Given that the letter agreement is an attempt to establish a uniform approach to consulting agreements, it must exact a price for this uniformity. The price exacted is flexibility to tailor an agreement to the specific situation. Therefore, in order that a form agreement not be overused and that the resort to the form not replace analysis of a unique situation, good management practices may dictate that an agreement such as this be limited to assignments with an estimated amount not to exceed $5,000 in total compensation or be limited to duties able to be performed in a specific period of time, say eighteen months, or some combination of these criteria. For consulting relationships in excess of $5,000 or longer than eighteen months, the formal contract for consulting services is appropriate.

## WHY THE LETTER AGREEMENT SHOULD BE IN WRITING

Regardless of the duration of the appointment, the kind of services provided, or the compensation paid, no consulting relationship should be entered into without some kind of written agreement. From a legal point of view, certain agreements cannot be enforced without some written documents that constitute evidence of the agreement between the parties. Some examples of these agreements are those relating to real property, agreements to be performed over a long period of time, and agreements that involve the payment upon the occurence of certain contingencies. From a management point of view, without a written memorandum between the parties indicating the nature of the services performed, the parties simply are asking for trouble. One must presume that all agreements have been entered into in good faith. Good faith at the beginning, however, does not take into account intervening problems and events. Memories are not infallible, and one person's recollection of a conversation may not be the same as someone else's.

A more common management problem that arises from an oral agreement concerns the nature of the services to be provided. Suppose, for example, that an officer of a corporation retains a consultant orally. That consultant is to work directly with a junior officer or with the officer in question on a project. Over the course of the project, the consultant receives differing instructions from the officer for whom he or she is working, or from superior officers. Is the consultant to treat these directions as modifications in the contract or as a new contract between the consultant and the corporation, or is the consultant to disregard them? These are the kinds of problems that can arise when the relationship is oral only.

## ADAPTING THE LETTER AGREEMENT TO PARTICULAR NEEDS

In adapting a form of letter agreement, not all of the clauses in the agreement may be needed in every case. For example, if a clause deals with the provision of working facilities and this is not within the contemplation of the parties, there is no reason to include such language in the letter agreement. If the agreement is preprinted, the unnecessary sections should be crossed out and the changes initialed. When the agreement is submitted to the consultant, the consultant should initial the changes in the text as well. This applies to any changes in a printed or typewritten form. As a general rule, all additions or deletions, even if handwritten, should be initialed or signed by both parties.

Needless to say, no form agreement can provide for all contingencies. In preparing any agreement, one should not be a slave to any form but should think through the issues involved using the form as a checklist as well as a model. Often it is useful to have a form of agreement available to a corporation as a basis upon which it may contract generally, by providing a first set of conditions

and clauses upon which negotiations can be centered as well as upper-level management control over the contracting powers of subordinates. For these reasons,
alternative clauses can be provided for those in the letter agreement to deal with
other commonly recurring situations. One alternative, for example, may provide
for retaining a consultant for a specific period of time by changing paragraphs 1
and 3(a).

For retention of consultant for a specific period:

1. *Term.* I am pleased to confirm your appointment as a consultant to
_____ (The Corporation) for the period _____ to _____.

For retention of consultant for a specific period:

3. (a) Your compensation will be at the rate of $_____ per month
for all work performed hereunder. You will be paid at the same
time you are reimbursed for approved expenses under paragraph
3 (b) below.

The first alternate paragraph is self-explanatory. The paragraph replacing paragraph 3 (a) provides that compensation will be paid monthly in conjunction with
the expense reimbursement. In such a situation, the parties should be aware that
no extension of the agreement is possible except in writing. The corporation
should be aware that if the consultant continues to perform services for it after
the term of the agreement, the parties may not be operating under this agreement; they may find that their practices, as well as the common law, will modify
the agreement they both believe exists between them.

## Duration and Services

The first matter the letter agreement should deal with is the term of the appointment of the consultant. Consultants may be appointed or retained on a number
of different bases. One common basis is to serve in connection with a particular
project the corporation is engaged in. This project is presumably of a fixed duration or otherwise identifiable. In such case, paragraph 1 shown in the letter agreement is appropriate.

1. *Term.* I am pleased to confirm your appointment as a consultant to _____ (The Corporation) to serve in connection with the _____ project.

If the project is not easily identifiable, the consultant should not be hired by reference to the project but should be retained on another basis, say for a specific term. The discussion of the letter agreement assumes that the consultant is retained to serve in connection with a particular project, probably the most common situation.

The matter of the nature of the services of the consultant is very important. All too often, parties to a consulting relationship leave the nature of the services to be specified after the fact and fall back on using form language, talking in terms of directions to be given by the corporation and specific matters to be agreed upon at a later date. This is unsatisfactory and, as a matter of law, may in fact be unenforceable for being too vague or for not being evidence of the entering into of a contract by the parties. One way to handle this is to have the parties set forth a specific description of the work or services to be performed. This may be prepared in advance by the consultant, by the corporation, or as a result of the process of negotiation. Use of an attachment enables the corporation to utilize a form of letter agreement, preprinted if necessary, adaptable to virtually all situations. In addition, it deals with the situation in which consultants may submit a written bid; this bid becomes the description of services or work, as Exhibit A. Alternatively, consultants may submit an unsolicited proposal, which the corporation may wish to accept. In either case, only the description of work or services should be attached and not any terms or conditions that often accompany a proposal and are covered by the letter agreement, such as reimbursement for expenses and treatment of confidential information. If the attachment, Exhibit A, includes language on such points, then a conflict has been created because language has been incorporated on the same topic covered in the agreement but providing for different treatment. Unless a clause is inserted in the letter agreement that limits the effect of Exhibit A to the description of work or services, it is better to extract the specific description from the proposal or bid and delete all other language.

## EXHIBIT A

This is attached to and made a part of the Letter Agreement, dated
_____, 198 ____ between _____
(the Corporation) and _____ (the Consultant).

The Consultant will evaluate the record-keeping systems currently
utilized by the Corporation in the Corporation's material's handling
division pertaining to inventory control and will recommend
improvements in these systems.
    The evaluation will include, but not be limited to:
1.  A review of the records being generated on a regular basis.
2.  Evaluation of storage and access systems.
3.  Examination of long-term retention systems and standards.
    The written recommendations must include specific
recommendations on at least the following:
A.  Which records being generated can be eliminated.
B.  In what form should the current records be kept, i.e. hard copy,
    microfilm, and/or computer memory.
C.  How long should records be kept available in the work place.
D.  When current records should be sent to long term storage and in
    what form.
E.  When current records can be destroyed.
F.  Which records, if any, must be kept indefinitely.
The written recommendations include evaluations of the costs and
benefits of implementing each or all of the changes recommended.
    The written recommendations are to be delivered to the
Corporation within 120 days of the date of the Letter Agreement.


Paragraph 2 also provides that the work or services to be performed by the
consultant may be changed from time to time by letter requests sent to the consultant. This kind of clause deals with only very narrow changes; any broad
changes in the nature of the work or services performed should be treated as an
amendment to the contract.

2. *Services.* You shall perform such work or services as are set forth in Exhibit A, attached hereto and specifically made a part of this Agreement. The work or services to be performed by you may be changed by the Corporation from time to time by letter requests sent to you. You shall keep the Corporation informed of the progress of any work being performed under this Agreement.

Language such as paragraph 2 should not be treated as an open-ended invitation to the corporation to add or delete major responsibilities under this agreement. This clause also is appropriate when a consultant is retained on an open-ended basis and the corporation utilizes formal written requests to activate the agreement, such as when a corporation retains an advertising consultant in order to have the advertising consultant available. The corporation pays the consultant a fixed sum, in the nature of an option, and also pays the consultant on a work-performed basis. The corporation activates the contract by sending a letter to the consultant requesting that he review certain advertising materials or plan an advertising campaign. In that case the work may be adjusted or even assigned by letter request. The term and compensation clauses must be akin to the alternative paragraphs 1 and 3 (a), providing for retention on a continuing basis.

For retention of consultant on a continuing basis:

1. *Appointment.* I am pleased to confirm your appointment as a consultant to _____ (The Corporation).

For retention of consultant on a continuing basis:

3.a. Your compensation will be at the rate of $_____ per (hour) (day) and will be based on the submission of Certification of Work Forms (enclosed) on a monthly basis. You will be paid at the same time you are reimbursed for approved expenses under paragraph 3(b) below.

## Progress of Work

Paragraph 2 provides that the consultant must keep the corporation informed of the progress of any work being performed under the agreement. This clause has several purposes, as listed below.

**1.** It keeps the corporation aware of progress on the project to make sure that the consultant is working on it on a regular basis.

**2.** It forces the consultant to keep this project or his relationship to the corporation constantly in mind so that his or her time does not become allocated elsewhere.

**3.** It enables the corporation to control the consultant if the consultant is working in the wrong direction, is incurring extraordinarily large expenses, or is devoting excessive amounts of time to the project.

**4.** It makes both parties aware of the existence of the relationship. This is most important when a corporation retains a consultant on a continuing basis and does not utilize the consultant for an extended period of time. The consultant may use this clause to keep the corporation apprised of the fact that there is in fact still a contractual relationship between the two parties.

## Compensation and Expenses

Paragraph 3 deals with compensation and expenses. In the form letter agreement, subparagraph (a) establishes a set total fee for all work performed, payable upon satisfactory completion of the work. This enables the corporation to judge if the work is, in fact, satisfactory. Of course, this decision must be made in good faith. The clause cannot be used as a way of terminating the agreement to avoid paying the consultant. Other compensation patterns should be adjusted to fit the nature of the work performed, as discussed below in conjunction with the alternative clauses in the Appendix.

3. *Compensation and Expenses.*
   a. The Corporation will pay you a total fee of $_____ for all work performed hereunder on satisfactory completion of the work.
   b. You will receive reimbursement for the actual cost of reasonable expenses arising out of the work performed under this Agreement [not to exceed $_____], subject to the approval of the Corporation. You shall deliver an itemized statement to

the Corporation on a monthly basis that shows fully the work being performed under this Agreement and all related expenses. The Corporation will pay you the amount of any authorized expenses within thirty (30) days of the receipt of the itemized statement of all expenses, submitted together with receipts for all hotel, car rental, air fare, and other transportation expenses and for all other expenses of $25.00 or more.

Paragraph 3 (b) provides for the reimbursement of expenses and the submission of invoices. If the consultant is to receive reimbursement for expenses, the terms of that reimbursement must be spelled out. This clause makes the consultant's expenses subject to the corporation's approval and payable on delivery of a monthly itemized, receipted statement. This statement also shows the work being performed under the agreement to allow the corporation to decide whether the expenses are reasonable. The corporation is obligated to make prompt payment to the consultant. If the corporation wishes, the total expenses under the contract may be limited by the language shown in the brackets. If the corporation wishes to impose specific expense limitations, such as not permitting first-class travel, they should be specified here, or reference should be made to a written set of company expense and entertainment standards given to the consultant. If such standards exist, this agreement may read as follows: ''You will receive reimbursement for the actual cost of reasonable expenses arising out of the work performed under this agreement in accord with the written standards of the corporation, attached as Exhibit B hereto and specifically made a part of this agreement.'' If the corporation provides certain benefits, such as trip insurance for the consultants as a matter of course, the consultant should be informed of this and should not be permitted to bill the corporation for these expenses on his own. The consultant then should be given necessary beneficiary and enrollment forms to complete. Care should be taken, however, not to offer to the consultant those benefits that are strictly employee benefits, as the consultant is not an employee and must not be treated as one for liability and other reasons discussed earlier.

## Working Facilities

Paragraph 4 discusses the question of working facilities. Some consultants will have to work on the corporation's premises. This may be a consulting engineer who has to examine a particular structure or progress on a particular job. Or it may be a management consultant coming in to evaluate work-flow processing and related issues in one part of the corporation. In these situations, the consultant needs a place to work and certain services provided by the corporation. If the corporation provides these, paragraph 4 should be adopted.

4. *Working Facilities.* You will be furnished with such facilities and services as shall be suitable for your position and adequate for the performance of your duties under this Agreement.

If the corporation does not intend to provide facilities and services at all, language should be inserted here to make this clear.

## Reports and Work Products

Paragraph 5 covers a matter rarely dealt with in consulting agreements but one of increasing importance, namely reports and work products.

5. *Reports.* Any and all reports, manuscripts, and any other work product, whether completed or not, that are prepared or developed by you as a part of the work under this Agreement shall be the property of the Corporation and shall be turned over to the Corporation promptly at the Corporation's request or at the termination of this Agreement, whichever is earlier.

When a management consultant is brought in to study a problem, his work product, in fact some of his performance under the agreement, may be in the form of a written report. After the report is delivered and accepted, the contract has been fulfilled and the relationship is ended. A problem arises when, for any number of reasons, performance cannot be completed and the parties wish to terminate the relationship. If the corporation has expended monies, it should have a right to the work in progress, whether completed or not. Without this clause, it is not certain that the corporation has a right to such materials. This clause gives the corporation the right to any and all reports, manuscripts, and any other work products, completed or not, that have been prepared or developed by the consultant as part of his or her work under the agreement. By inserting this clause, the consultant is on notice that such materials must be kept separate from that of other projects. This is particularly critical when a consultant is to prepare a survey of studies in a certain field and then is unable to complete the project. Even the partial notes of what the consultant has reviewed unsuccessfully may be of assistance to the corporation or another consultant in completing the project. Paragraph 5 also enables a corporation to establish whether a consultant has in fact worked under the agreement, if there should be a dispute regarding compensation upon termination or breach of contract. Even if the work of the consultant consists of providing a service rather than a report, these materials should be collected and received by the corporation. In the case of a consulting engineer, for example, his notes may be important to the corporation in the event of a lawsuit against the corporation arising out of the project. In such a situation, the agreement may stipulate that the consulting engineer will keep the originals of his notes and provide the corporation with a legible copy; this may protect the corporation if there were a lawsuit arising out of the work the engineer inspected and the engineer were not available to testify and validate his or her records.

## Independent Contractor

Paragraph 6 establishes the relationship between the corporation and the consultant.

6. *Independent Contractor.* You shall exercise control over the means and manner in which you perform any work requested hereunder, and in all respects your relationship to the Corporation shall be that of an independent contractor serving as a consultant and not as an employee.

The consultant is not an employee or agent but an independent contractor. The essence of this status is that the independent contractor exercises control over the way in which he or she performs the work assigned. To the extent that the corporation tells the consultant how to do the work, the corporation is transforming the relationship into that of employer to employee. Mere language cannot protect the corporation in a lawsuit by a third party. Too many people mistakenly believe that using such language, whether it is followed or not, results in legal protection. This is wrong. This language establishes the relationship between the parties, but in order for a corporation to prove that the relationship is that of an independent contractor it must rely on the fact of the relationship. Paragraph 6 is a direction. It tells the parties how they should treat each other; if they treat each other in this manner, the relationship will be that of an independent contractor.

## Termination

Termination as provided for in paragraph 7 is fairly standard.

> 7. *Termination.* This Agreement may be terminated upon thirty (30) days written notice by either party.

The corporation should determine whether it wishes the agreement to be terminated on notice or not. It may wish the agreement to be terminated upon its notice, particularly when the agreement is for a period of time and not for a particular project. It is unlikely that a corporation will want the consultant to be able to terminate this on less than thirty days' notice. In fact, the corporation may wish that the agreement may be terminated by the consultant on thirty days' notice only if the consultant provides an acceptable substitute to the corporation who will assume the responsibilities of the consultant under this project.

## Confidentiality of Information

Paragraph 8 of the letter agreement is a carefully drawn provision dealing with confidentiality of information.

> 8. *Confidential Information.* You agree that for the term of your appointment hereunder and for two (2) years thereafter, that you will not disclose to any person, firm, or corporation any confidential information regarding the Corporation, its businesses, directors, officers, and employees.

This clause is extremely important and should be the subject of careful consideration. In it the consultant agrees that during the term of the agreement and for two years after its expiration the consultant will not disclose any confidential information concerning the corporation, its businesses, directors, officers, and employees. One danger in drafting such a clause is that there is a tendency to make it too broad. The courts may hold unenforceable a contract providing that confidential information will not be disclosed forever. When the clause is unenforceable, there is no protection at all.

In some states, certain kinds of business information, such as customer lists, are protected by statute from disclosure. These protected business secrets include a range of data and information narrower than confidential information. If there is specific sensitive information that the corporation is concerned may be disclosed to its detriment, this clause can be modified to deal specifically with such information. In revising it, care should be taken not to make this clause too broad, or it may fall.

The retention of a consultant for a continuing or indefinite period of time raises a problem in dealing with confidential information. The confidential-information clause in the letter agreement is keyed to two years from the end of the agreement. Under a continuing relationship, there is no specific term, so the agreement does not end. If the consultant is performing no service for a period of time, it could tie his or her hands unfairly. Paragraph 8 on confidential information therefore should be modified as shown to provide that the two years begin from the date the consultant gives or receives notice of termination.

For retention of consultant on a continuing basis:

8. *Confidential Information.* You agree that while you are serving as a consultant to the Corporation and for two (2) years after you have given or received notice of termination under paragraph 7 above you will not disclose to any person, firm, or corporation any confidential information regarding the Corporation, its businesses, directors, officers, and employees.

Alternate paragraph 8 clearly stipulates that the consultant and/or the corporation, after the consultant's services have not been used for some time, will give formal notice to terminate the agreement. The corporation should make clear to the consultant that the termination of such a relationship is required for this and other administrative purposes and may have nothing to do with the ability of the consultant or the satisfactory performance of his or her services.

## Nonassignability

Paragraph 9 makes the contract nonassignable.

9. *Nonassignable.* This Agreement is personal in nature and is not assignable by you or by the Corporation.

Without such a clause, the consultant or the corporation can transfer the agreement to another person and provide that that person perform its duties under the agreement. In most of these situations, the party assigning the agreement serves as guarantor of the performance for the party to whom the agreement is assigned. Given that a consultant very often is hired based upon his or her specialized knowledge or expertise, assignment of the agreement may be undesirable from the corporation's point of view. Without a nonassignment clause, the potential assignability of the contract is uncertain. Here, as in other situations, sound management dictates that questions be resolved without resort to legal counsel after the fact by negotiation and drafting before the fact.

The letter agreement as prepared stipulates that the corporation does not wish to have the agreement assigned by the consultant to another individual. It also stipulates that the consultant has agreed to perform certain services for a particular employer. In this age of corporate shells, general and limited partnerships, and special trust arrangements for financial purposes, the corporation entering into the consulting agreement may not be the corporation for which the services ultimately are to be performed. This may be the result of a formal corporate decision that all agreements of a certain size are entered into by, say, the parent corporation, thus depriving subsidiaries of the power to make certain kinds of agreements. In such a case, the agreement can provide that the consultant is performing services for a specifically described corporation that is a subsidiary of the corporation with whom he has negotiated this agreement.

Another common situation occurs when the corporation retaining the consultant engages in a new business venture. As such, the corporation later may find that the instrumentality for the project may be a new subsidiary or affiliated company or a limited partnership in which the corporation is a participant. In such cases, the consultant logically should be performing his services for this new enterprise, which may not even be in existence at the time the agreement is signed. The first revised paragraph 9 deals with this problem.

Transferable from the corporation to a related enterprise:

9. *Assignments.* Performance by you under this Agreement is personal in nature, and this Agreement is not assignable by you. The Corporation may assign this Agreement to any subsidiary, affiliate, or related enterprise upon written notice to you.

This clause provides that the agreement may not be assigned by the consultant, but that the corporation may assign it to a subsidiary, affiliate, or other related corporation, partnership, or business entity.

From the corporation's point of view, it wishes to assure adequate performance of its assignments. A second alternate paragraph 9 provides that the consultant may assign the agreement to any person, including a corporation, "of equal responsibility" to the consultant.

Assignable by the consultant:

9. *Assignments.* With the prior written consent of the Corporation, you may assign this Agreement and the benefits and obligation hereunder to any person, including a corporation, of equal responsibility to you. The consent of the Corporation may not be withheld unreasonably.

This, of course, requires that the consultant disclose to the corporation substantial information about the assignee to permit the corporation to determine its responsibility. This disclosure includes who owns the assignee, if it is a corporation, and who will be administering and performing under the agreement. The clause provides that the consent of the corporation may not be withheld unreasonably, thereby providing some flexibility to the consultant. It is not impossible that the corporation may wish to withhold its consent unreasonably, but including a clause stating this, or deleting the last sentence in the second revised paragraph 9, may get the consultant-corporate relationship off to a very awkward start.

## Arbitration of Disputes

Paragraph 10 provides that disputes under this agreement will be settled by arbitration under the auspices of the American Arbitration Association (AAA). The blank should be filled in with the city and state of the nearest regional office of the AAA. A complete list of these offices may be found in the Appendix. The last sentence is designed to assure that either party seeking arbitration may begin the process without having to convince the other party to move to arbitration. The desirability of arbitration over other remedies is discussed further in chapter 8.

10. *Arbitration.* Any controversy or claim arising out of, or relating to this Agreement or the breach thereof shall be settled at _____ in accordance with the rules then obtaining of the American Arbitration Association, and judgment upon the award may be entered in any court having jurisdiction thereof. This Agreement constitutes the voluntary submission of both parties to such arbitration.

## Integration Clause

Paragraph 11 is an integration clause.

11. *Entire Agreement.* This letter, including Exhibit A, contains the entire agreement of the parties. It may not be changed orally but only by an agreement signed by the party against whom enforcement of any waiver, change, modification, extension, or discharge is sought.

At this point, sound management dictates that the parties entering into the agreement really have incorporated all of their understandings, terms, and conditions into the document. If this letter agreement does not contain the entire agreement of the parties, it should be revised to include the entire agreement. The second sentence protects both parties against oral modification. In the case of the consultant, it avoids the problem of dealing with several individuals at the corporate level who may be giving contradictory or new instructions for assignments not covered by the agreement. In the case of the corporation, it protects against misunderstandings with the consultant and makes sure that the instructions given to the consultant are thought out fully and within the bounds of the agreement.

## Closing of the Letter Agreement

Paragraph 12 closes the agreement and provides that the corporation retain the complete agreement as signed by both parties. A copy is provided for the consultant's records. If the consultant desires, there is no reason not to provide him or her with a signed agreement as well. The two documents must be identical.

12. *Approval.* I trust that the terms of this appointment meet with your

approval. If so, please indicate this by signing a copy of this letter and returning it to the Corporation. An additional copy of this letter is enclosed for your records.

## Description of the Work to Be Performed

Exhibit A, the description of the work to be performed, is extremely important. Although the agreement is a legal instrument between the parties, the agreement preparation and execution may serve as a checklist for the parties to assure that complete agreement has been reached and that both parties clearly understand the duties, obligations, and responsibilities imposed on each of them. Exhibit A, the description of the work to be performed, is perhaps the most difficult part of the contract to prepare and certainly the most important.

This document should not contain any additional clauses or conditions, only a pure description of the work. Including extraneous matters will only cause problems in interpreting the agreement between the parties. After the specific language of Exhibit A has been agreed upon by both parties, it should be dated and labeled to indicate that it is a part of the letter agreement between the corporation and the consultant. The parties to the agreement should initial or sign the exhibit, which should be attached to the letter agreement.

In no case should the preparation or execution of Exhibit A be left to some later date. First, this omission may render the letter agreement void, since the parties have not reached an agreement on the specific subject matter of the contract. Second, this leaves open for collateral negotiation issues that properly may be a part of the agreement. Third, the agreement is attempting to incorporate by reference a document that did not exist at its execution; this is not sound legal practice. Fourth, if the parties are unable to arrive at an agreement upon a statement of the work, postponing it may only serve to conceal or suppress deeper, more fundamental disagreements on the nature of the work and the work product; this in itself should be a warning to the corporation.

# CHAPTER SEVEN

# Master Consulting Contract

## WHEN AN ELABORATE CONTRACT IS NECESSARY

Although a letter agreement like that discussed in chapter 6 probably is satisfactory for most consulting relationships, many times the relationship contemplated will be over a long period of time, involve substantial amounts of money, or involve matters of such importance to the retaining corporation that a more elaborate consulting agreement should be prepared. The difference between the master consulting contract and the letter agreement is a matter of scope. The master contract covers more subjects in greater detail. A corporation could, of course, add clauses from the master contract to the letter agreement to cover specific issues, such as copyrights, not covered in the letter agreement.

In using the model consulting contract included in the Appendix together with alternative clauses, the corporation always should be aware that an agreement of this sort serves two purposes: it forces the parties to think through and cover all areas of importance to them, and it provides sample tested language that may be used to handle these points. If the sample language does not cover the points in the manner to which the parties have agreed, they can modify the language very simply. In any case, they have language with which to start.

## HOW TO ADAPT THE FORM IN THIS BOOK

The most effective way to use a form contract is as a checklist. The clauses themselves are straightforward and reflect an attempt to create a working relationship between the parties and to deal with problems obvious to them at the beginning of the contract, as well as those problems that experience has shown can arise during the performance of the contract or in the event of a falling out between the parties during the term of the contract. Although clauses should not be adopted as mere protective armor, the use of a clause to cover a portion of the relationship or to end the relationship between the parties is not without merit. The contract is designed to reflect all the elements of the agreement between the parties; that is the purpose of the integration clause. To do this the parties should cover even those circumstances they do not believe are likely to occur. Once the contract has been signed, the parties then will be faced with having to resolve an issue when it arises and when its resolution becomes a matter of importance to one of the parties.

One matter that can be dealt with only by illustration is compensation. A consultant's compensation can be as varied as the project on which the consultant is working. The forms of agreements show daily billing, as well as fixed fee, with and without reimbursement of expenses. There are many other forms, such as cost-plus-percentage contracts. In such a contract, the consultant is paid all of the costs involved plus some percentage of that as an override. An additional clause may provide that a consultant is paid a percentage of the money the consultant saves or recaptures for the corporation. In both cases, the contract should define precisely the basis upon which the compensation for the consultant is being paid. In the case of a cost-plus contract, which costs are included and which excluded? In the case of the recapture clause, how will the parties calculate the money saved and over what period of time? The money saved by a corporation for reviewing communications services can be evaluated daily, monthly, weekly, yearly, or longer. Needless to say, the period of time used to measure the savings will affect the compensation of the consultant radically.

Anyone using this form or any other form in this book should feel free to make changes reflecting the intent of the parties. Simply inserting or removing the word "not," for example, can indicate the intent of the parties and can convert a clause that does not meet the parties' needs into one that does. There is no magic in the language of a contract. The language used in contracts reflects the accumulated experience of businesses, lawyers, and the courts. The key is clarity of expression. If the parties to a contract want different or additional provisions, they should not hesitate to include them. The criterion should be that the clause delineates the rights and responsibilities of the parties to the contract and can be understood by a third party.

In sum, the contract is an expression of the agreement of the parties and a true management tool. A well-drawn contract will eliminate problems and not cause them. There is an old saying among corporation lawyers that if a contract has to be interpreted by a court, someone made a mistake in drafting it. This saying reflects the commercial reality that a well-drafted contract that memorializes negotiations between the parties covering all facets of an agreement will lead to an effective, efficient performance of services on both sides and will minimize the likelihood that the parties ever will suffer a dispute. As indicated in chapter 8, the contract itself may provide ways in which the dispute may be handled.

## WHAT THE CONTRACT SHOULD COVER

### The Parties to the Contract

The preamble identifies the parties and sets the context of the agreement. For easy preparation of a contract, abbreviate the name of the retaining corporation in some way. In the form of the contract in the Appendix, the company is known as "The Service Company" and is referred to in the contract as "TSC." Another way may be simply to leave a blank, insert the name of the corporation, and refer to it throughout as the "Corporation."

This contract sets forth the terms and conditions under which The Service Company ("TSC") proposes to use the services of _____, Inc. ("Consultant") from time to time to perform work or services ("Work") as described in work requests from TSC's representative hereunder, all such Work to be performed on the following basis and subject to the following terms and conditions:

Throughout the contract, the first time a specialized term is used, it is followed by a word or phrase in parentheses or quotes, which is the way lawyers' shorthand is designed to encompass a repeated idea of a concept. As a matter of style, lawyers tend to capitalize some of these words to indicate throughout the agreement that they carry some special meaning, such as the word "Work," which describes the vast range of services covered by the agreement.

### Scope of the Work

This form of agreement is designed to cover an ongoing relationship in which the corporation sends written work requests to the consultant to cover contingencies in the future. In general, the scope of the work to be performed by the consultant should be stated as specifically as possible. If the work statement is put in general terms in the preamble, it can be defined further by the use of work requests provided for in paragraph 1 by changing the phrase "as described in work requests" to read "as more fully described in work requests." Whenever possible, time of performance and standards of performance should be established in the agreement rather than in the work requests.

The necesssity for clarity and precision in the description of the work to be done is illustrated by a contract dispute with the federal government. In 1976, the U.S. Office of Education (OE) sought a consultant to develop an interpretive structure model based on "an analysis of resources for environmental education and studies." The contractor selected submitted a forty-five-page proposal, which was accepted. The consultant then delivered his first progress report. The OE characterized these papers "unintelligible" and decided to terminate the contract on the grounds the consultant had defaulted. The OE also sought to force the consultant to repay the money he had already collected. Ultimately, the OE agreed to pay the consultant about 50 percent of the total contract price to settle the case and get out of the contract. The reason for the OE's change of position was a lack of a clear understanding of the work to be done. As the OE's own contract officer put it, "How can we say they defaulted when it was never clear what we were expecting?"

## Work Requests

Paragraph 1 is designed to carry out the concept of the written work request by stating that the corporation may request the consultant or employees of the consultant to perform the work. This gives the corporation the power to designate specific individuals to carry on specially designated services.

> 1. TSC shall have the right from time to time to request in writing that Consultant or certain employees of Consultant perform consulting work (the "Work") for TSC, provided, however, Consultant shall have the right to refuse any work request by notifying TSC within ten (10) days after receipt of the work request.

If it is not important that specific employees be identified, then the phrase "or certain employees of consultant" can be deleted. The proviso indicates that the consultant has the right to reject work requests in order to protect himself. Essentially the consultant is entering into an open-ended relationship and must have the right to manage the time of his personnel to handle several clients effectively.

Optional paragraph 1 defines the work to be done by the consultant when it has been agreed upon in advance by the corporation and the consultant. They prepare a statement of the work which is attached to the contract and incorporated in it. The use of an attachment permits the corporation to use a standard form of contract which can be adapted to almost all situations. The uses and drawbacks of this are discussed in more detail in chapter 4.

1. All of the work or service to be performed by Consultant for TSC under this Agreement (hereinafter collectively referred to as the "Work") are more fully described in Schedule A, attached hereto and by this reference specifically made a part hereof.

Because the master contract is designed for longer, more costly assignments, the corporation and consultant may find that the work agreed upon at the beginning needs to be changed. If the parties mutually agree on changes in the assignment, schedule A can be amended or replaced. If the parties replace or amend schedule A, they should sign each new page of the schedule.

Paragraph 2 provides that all of the work requests will be made only by a specified individual deemed the representative for the performance of this agreement. The paragraph is designed to protect both sides against the dangers described earlier of conflicting sets of directions, untoward interference by different levels of corporate officers, and other management problems in the interface between the consultant and the corporation.

2. Unless TSC shall specify otherwise in writing, all requests for Work to be performed hereunder shall be made in writing by _____, who shall, in all respects, be considered TSC's Representative hereunder. In the event of ____'s absence or incapacity, ____ is designated TSC's Alternate Representative. Consultant shall keep TSC or its Representatives informed of the progress of the Work being performed hereunder.

Since the designated individual, the "representative," is an important person, in a long-term contract it is wise to specify an alternate representative in order that the project is not delayed due to the absence of the designated representative. This designated representative under paragraph 2 is the person to whom progress reports of the work are made. In an extraordinarily long and complicated project, it may be necessary for the corporation to add additional language stating that it may designate such additional individuals to serve as alternate or substitute representatives; the designation should be made in writing and delivered to the consultant. This is extremely formal and is probably only necessary in the most lengthy, complicated, and expensive projects.

## SCHEDULE A TO AGREEMENT BETWEEN TSC AND _____
Dated _____,198__

The work performed under this Agreement will be on a billing-rate basis in accordance with the following rate structure:

| *Number of days* | *Rate per Day* |
|---|---|
| _____ | $_____ |

Partial days will be prorated on an hourly basis.

The above rates cover all direct labor. Expenses incurred, such as travel, subsistence, copying, etc., will be billed at cost.

### Compensation and Costs

Paragraph 3 and schedules A and B deal with the question of fees and costs. There are many ways in which the consultant may be compensated for his services. For example, the consultant may be paid a fixed fee, in which case paragraph 3 and schedule A will state that the consultant, for performing his services, will be paid a fixed fee.

3. Attached hereto as Schedule A, and by this reference specifically made a part hereof, is a schedule of fees and other costs to be paid by TSC in connection with any Work that may be performed by Consultant for TSC. Schedule A may be updated from time to time by Consultant whenever it becomes necessary to change the fees set forth therein. Whenever such a revised Schedule A has been received by TSC, the revised Schedule A shall replace the prior Schedule A and by this reference shall become a part of this Agreement between TSC and Consultant, provided, however, no revision of Schedule A shall be in effect regarding any work requests then outstanding.

The consultant also may bill the corporation on an hourly basis for services rendered. In this situation, an hourly rate for the personnel, either as a group or individually, should be agreed upon unless the parties wish to provide that the services rendered by the consultant will be billed to the corporation at the consultant's usual rates. Although this is common practice, it may not be desirable. The corporation may not know what rates are until it has received its first bill. To avoid misunderstandings, the parties at least should be aware of these rates prior to the rendering of the first bill or the performance of any services under this agreement. A third manner of compensation may be a cost-plus contract, where the consultant bills through the services of its personnel on a cost basis, calculated on the basis of their annual salary. The consultant will pay for other services, with the consent of the corporation, and will be paid a management service fee in the form of an override or percentage add-on. Finally, the consultant may be paid on the basis of some contingency, that is on the basis of, say, 25 percent of the amount saved the corporation by the consultant's activities over the term of the contract. In any case, the parties should deal with two items: fees and costs. As a rule the parties should leave nothing to implication. If the consultant is not to be reimbursed any costs, paragraph 3 should specify this. If the consultant is to receive reimbursement for only some costs, the contract should state so. Paragraph 3 incorporates by reference a schedule of fees and other costs to be paid by the corporation. This schedule of costs can be inclusive or limited, as the parties desire. The form of contract provides that the consultant may update the fee schedule from time to time. This is in contemplation of a long-term relationship, where the underlying fees charged by the consultant are expected to rise as its own personnel costs rise. To protect the corporation, any change in the fee schedule applies to new work requests, as opposed to existing or past work requests.

Optional paragraph 3 states that the consultant is paid a fixed monthly fee plus certain recoverable costs.

3. TSC shall pay Consultant for the Work performed hereunder the sum of (a) a fixed monthly fee of _____ thousand dollars ($      ) plus (b) recoverable costs as set forth in Schedule B attached hereto and by this reference made a part hereof.

The recoverable costs are set forth in schedule B, to be attached to the contract. Sample schedule B (Appendix) is an extremely broad, far-reaching schedule of recoverable costs. It is designed to pay the direct costs of the consultant for performing under this contract. This kind of broad-scale clause is used when the consultant is required to make a substantial dedication of employees and resources to a project for a prolonged period of time for a fixed fee. It is appropriate when the parties are in a relationship that can see additional or other duties added to a core set of duties, so that the consultant may be forced to add additional people to its payroll to meet the requests of the corporation. A recoverable costs schedule need not be so elaborate. The corporation and the consultant can agree to reimburse no costs or such costs as they specify. Schedule B gives the corporation the opportunity to use a form agreement but to gear its payment for services and expenses to the particular circumstances.

## Billing Procedure

Paragraph 4(a) is different from the billing procedure statement discussed earlier but not uncommon in practice. It requires itemized statements in contemplation of a relationship in which the hiring corporation is paying the consultant on a time basis for the work the consultant has done. The statement also requires an itemization of the authorized expenses. These expenses, if permitted, should be defined as the expenses authorized by paragraph 3. If other expenses are authorized on some other basis, that basis should be incorporated here.

> 4. (a) TSC shall pay Consultant a fee for all Work performed hereunder, such fee to be calculated on the basis of the fees set forth in Schedule A, attached hereto. Itemized statements shall be delivered to TSC on a monthly basis and shall show fully the task being performed, the individual(s) performing the task, the title of such individual(s), and the man-days involved. Such statement shall also include, in itemized form, Consultant's authorized expenses arising out of its performance of the work requested by TSC. TSC agrees to pay Consultant the amount of such statements within thirty (30) days after receipt thereof, provided, however, Consultant shall notify TSC immediately in writing when the fees and authorized expenses arising out of its performance of the Work under any work request exceed $_____

Paragraph 4(a) also provides that the corporation will pay the consultant promptly to avoid long outstanding bills. In a long-term relationship, cash flow from both sides can be an important issue. The last sentence in paragraph 4(a) is an addition designed to protect the corporation from requesting excessively expensive assignments. It sets a threshold; when the total cost of a project or subproject exceeds a certain amount, the consultant must inform the corporation.

This is a modification of a common corporate restriction on expenditures or authorizations. It makes sense to say that if an officer in a corporation cannot authorize a contract in excess of, say, ten thousand dollars, then he may be limited in the work requests he can transmit to a consultant; this ensures that these work requests (which from a financial point of view are akin to new contracts) will not exceed the threshold. If the parties are not concerned about this, the clause can be eliminated. Paragraph 4(b) covers additional performance not contemplated by the parties.

> 4. (b) In addition to the basic fee and costs herein agreed to be paid to the Consultant for Work hereunder, TSC shall pay the Consultant the direct fees and authorized costs, as defined in Schedule A, incurred by the Consultant in performing any additional work or services requested in writing by TSC's Representative and not required to be performed by the Consultant under this Agreement.

Paragraph 4(b) assumes that the parties have retained a consultant to work in conjunction with a particular project and that the parties have, through work requests, specified the scope of the consultant's work. If the additional work substantially different from that already undertaken under the contract is requested, the parties have resort to this clause. It sets forth that the consultant may be available for additional services but is not required to be so.

Optional paragraph 4 provides that the consultant deliver monthly statements to the corporation. These statements are designed to provide information to the corporation regarding the expenses and costs to date and to indicate the people involved in the project. This serves as a control device to avoid running up excessive costs. It also enables the corporation to prepare more adequate evaluations of the consulting firm and its employees for its own future use. Paragraph 4 provides for prompt payment to the consultant of its monthly statements. This is particularly important when the consultant is seeking reimbursement for substantial costs and expenses.

> 4. Statements shall be delivered to TSC on a monthly basis and shall show the nature of the Work performed, the individual(s) performing the task, the title of such individual(s) and the man-days involved. Such statements shall also include, in itemized form, Consultant's

recoverable costs arising out of its performance of the Work. TSC agrees to pay Consultant the amount of such statements within fifteen (15) days after receipt thereof.

## Work Product

Paragraph 5 is a work-product clause designed to accomplish several ends. At the completion of a contract, the corporation that has paid for a project should have full rights to all the work product it has paid for. This paragraph clearly sets forth that the reports or the work products are to be delivered to the party that paid for them.

> 5. Any and all reports, manuscripts, or any other Work product, whether completed or not, which are prepared or developed by Consultant as part of the Work requested by TSC hereunder, shall be the property of TSC and shall be turned over to TSC promptly at TSC's request or at the termination of this agreement, whichever is earlier.

If for a number of reasons the parties are not able to complete the performance under the contract because of inability, intervening acts, or breach of contract, paragraph 5 gives the corporation the right to whatever work product the consultant has completed. This provision serves several functions. First, it assures that the company will be able to transfer what it has paid for to a replacement or successor consulting firm. Second, it serves as a form of control over the activities of the consultant. Often, corporations not used to using consultants are concerned that the consultants are in fact progressing on their work, as often there is no work product until the final report. The clause says that the company can request these materials be turned over to them. This gives the corporation a way to check on the progress of the consultant and enables it to feel more secure in paying for ongoing work by a consultant when it is unable to see a finished work product.

## Patents and Copyrights

Paragraph 6 is designed to handle the development of patentable or copyrightable processes or techniques.

6. Except as provided below, TSC shall have the right to and shall own any and all patentable or copyrightable inventions, processes, plans, or techniques, together with any applications for patents or copyrights and the patents and the copyrights that may issue thereunder, which are created, developed, or invented by Consultant or any of its employees as a result of or arising out of the Work requested by TSC hereunder. At TSC's request and expense, Consultant agrees to do or cause to be done all things necessary to enable TSC to require the full right to the use and ownership of any and all the rights and properties described hereinabove in this paragraph 6.

It provides that the corporation should receive the benefits of the work product since it has paid for the work. In addition, the consultant agrees to render all coöperation to assure that the corporation can apply for and receive appropriate patents or copyrights. This is required because the consultant, having developed the process, may, under statute, be the only person who has the right to file the application for patent or copyright. Although the corporation owns the process, it does not have the ability to protect it. The consultant therefore must agree to coöperate and render all services necessary. If the parties contemplate that the consultant will be doing specialized work, such as developing a media or advertising campaign that may produce trademarkable output, this clause should be amended to include all patentable, trademarkable, or copyrightable inventions.

## Confidential Information

Paragraph 7 is designed to deal with the sensitive area of confidential information, which must be discussed by the parties to an agreement very carefully.

7. In the performance of the Work, Consultant may acquire or be made aware of certain confidential information, in particular, but not limited to, confidential information relating to the work, regarding products, processes, and operations as well as present and contemplated activities of TSC. Consultant, its employees, and others whose services may be procured by Consultant to assist Consultant in the performance of the Work shall not divulge or disclose such confidential information to others without first having obtained specific written permission from TSC to do so. The term "confidential information"

as used herein shall mean information disclosed to Consultant by TSC or information obtained by Consultant for TSC in the course of performing the Work hereunder, excluding information previously known to Consultant or information that is publicly known (except through disclosure of Consultant in violation of this paragraph) or information that comes to Consultant by right from a third party without confidential commitment.

If the corporation is concerned about a certain kind of confidential information, it should specify in the last sentence of paragraph 7 that it means certain information, "including but not limited to" the category of information about which it is concerned, such as customer lists. This is important because many consultants must have access to extremely confidential information, in some cases information available to only a few employees and officers of the corporation. In fact, in performing consulting services the consultant may have access to classes of information that collectively are not available to anyone below the chief operating or chief executive officer. Thus, there must be a nondisclosure agreement. Without a nondisclosure agreement, the only protection the parties have is common-law or statutory protection of information generally known as business secrets. Business secrets are a narrower category of information than confidential information. Business secrets include customer lists, unpatented manufacturing processes, and instructions to marketing forces. Confidential information includes salary scales, development plans for new markets, studies on the possibility of acquisitions of industries in new fields, and other information that does not bear directly on the day-to-day business of the corporation. For this reason the parties should not rely on the few state statutes that protect narrow categories of business information but should handle it specifically here. If the consultant is to be given copies of particularly confidential materials that must be used off the premises of the corporation, such as salary schedules, the agreement may state that the corporation agrees to deliver this information to the consultant but that the consultant agrees not to make or retain any copies and to return it directly to the corporation.

Paragraph 17 attempts to protect the confidential information received by the consultant from outside disclosure for a period of years. It is impossible and improper to bind the consultant forever in its use of information received from the corporation. Various state laws and federal laws protect the corporation against the disclosure of certain business and trade secrets. The consultant may have access to materials not traditionally regarded as business secrets but, the disclosure of which may be damaging to the employing corporation. Paragraph 17 is designed to cover this. In establishing the number of years for which the agreement will apply, the parties should be realistic and deal with the potentially damaging nature of information to which the consultant may have access. Customer lists are one sensitive matter. It seems unlikely that a corporation will be concerned about revealing its customer lists five years after the fact. Certain kinds of confidential manufacturing processes, however, should be protected for longer periods of time. For example, there are corporations that do not patent formulas for soft drinks and snack foods. These trade secrets may have a long commercial life and should be protected by the contract for longer periods of time.

> 17. During the term of this Agreement, and for _____ years thereafter, Consultant shall not reveal to outside sources, without the written consent of TSC, any matters, the reveal of which may, in any manner, adversely affect TSC's business, unless required by law to do so.

Three to five years will cover most manufacturing and service industries in paragraph 17. To the extent that there are business and trade secrets of substantial value, the duration of this clause should be lengthened, but the parties should have memoranda supporting the reasons for such a long period of time in case it is challenged later.

### Indemnifications; Limitations of Liability

Paragraph 8 generally is regarded as an indemnity clause. This clause provides that if certain actions by the consultant under the agreement result in a lawsuit against the corporation, the consultant agrees to indemnify—that is repay or pay in advance—those costs and judgments so that the corporation is unharmed. This clause should be amended to include trademarks if paragraph 6 also covers trademarks.

> 8. Consultant shall save, indemnify, and hold TSC harmless from all liability, claims, suits, judgments, damages, and losses growing out of any infringement of any patent or patent rights or copyrights covering any equipment, machine, appliance, operation, or method of

operation practiced by Consultant, in the performance of the Work requested hereunder by TSC.

Paragraph 8 is extremely broad, but unless the parties wish to narrow the scope of indemnity, it must be prepared in the broadest terms. In addition to any wrongs committed by the consultant during the term of the contract, this clause covers activities that may arise thereafter. For example, if the company is involved in a copyright dispute about the work product produced by the consultant, this indemnity continues to provide some degree of protection for the corporation if the acts of the consultant in preparing the product resulted in a copyright violation. Although the consultant is an independent contractor, the product delivered to the company and which the corporation uses is the corporation's responsibility and not the consultant's. This clause will prevent a lawsuit and protect the corporation. It is not unforeseeable that the consultant will want an indemnification clause as well. The kind of clause in paragraph 8 is directed only at products and processes and not at general torts, as paragraph 10 is. Modification of paragraph 10 to provide that the corporation indemnify the consultant should be considered by the parties. It is hard to imagine the circumstances under which the consultant will want an indemnification clause, but if the parties agree, paragraph 10 is the better model.

> 10. Consultant shall indemnify and forever hold and save TSC harmless against any and all suits, causes of action, claims, liabilities, damages, or losses resulting from the acts or conduct of Consultant or its agents and employees, regardless of the character of the acts or conduct and asserted by anyone whomsoever, resulting from the performance of the Work requested hereunder, and for which the Consultant or its agents and employees are legally responsible.

Paragraph 10 is an indemnity clause covering all acts of the consultant and its employees that could result in lawsuits against the corporation. Although the corporation should not be liable for the acts of the consultant, it is a fact that corporations and other parties are sued every day for matters that are not their legal responsibility. Ultimately they will not have to pay damages in the form of a judgment, but they may incur substantial legal costs and other expenses in the preparation of the defense of such an action. Paragraph 10 provides that the consultant will repay the corporation for such costs arising out of activities for which the consultant or its agents and employees are held legally responsible. In this day of complex insurance issues, even the fact that the corporation has its legal defense covered by insurance does not eliminate the need to consider such a clause. If a company calls upon its errors and omissions insurance, directors' liability coverage, or one of the many other coverages available to it to defend an action, and the defense is successful, the corporation may have its insurance rates raised or its policy cancelled. Thus, even though it has not expended money for the defense of the case, it ultimately will pay for it.

Alternate paragraph 10 replaces paragraph 10 in the draft agreement. Alternate paragraph 10 limits the liability of the consultant to failure to perform in accordance with generally accepted professional standards and standards imposed by law.

> 10. Consultant shall be liable only for any failure to perform in accordance with generally accepted professional standards and the standards imposed by law. Consultant shall have no liability under this agreement unless the claim is made in writing within one (1) year after Consultant's completion of Work. Consultant's liability to TSC for any loss or damage arising out of or in connection with this Agreement from any cause, including Consultant's negligence, shall not exceed the total fixed monthly fees received by Consultant hereunder, and TSC hereby releases Consultant from any liability in excess of such amount. Under no circumstances shall Consultant be liable to TSC for any consequential or incidental damages including, but not limited to, loss of use or loss of profit, whether or not caused by Consultant's fault or negligence.

This kind of clause is appropriate when dealing with a consultant in what is generally regarded as a profession, namely law, medicine, accounting, or engineering. It states that the consultant has no liability unless there is a prompt transmission of a potential claim. Finally, it says that the consultant's liability under the contract cannot exceed its total income under the contract, to cover the special situation of the professional engaged in providing services in conjunction with a large project. For example, an architect may not be willing to provide certain consulting services in conjunction with the establishment of an industrial park if his liability is greater than his fee.

Alternate paragraph 14(b) is another clause directed at the liability of the parties. It provides that the parties are not liable for breach of contract or damages that occur due to factors beyond the reasonable control of the affected parties. This clause provides for the settlement of strikes and other lockouts; if one party suffers a strike, this is not considered an excuse for performance. Of course, the consultant and the corporation may wish to modify or delete this clause entirely, depending on the circumstances.

14. (b) Neither Party hereto shall be considered in default in the performance of its obligations hereunder to the extent that the performance of any such obligation is prevented or delayed by any cause, existing or future, beyond the reasonable control of the affected party, provided however, that the settlement of strikes and lockouts shall be entirely within the discretion of the Party having the difficulty.

## Status as Independent Contractor

Paragraph 9 is an expanded version of the independent-contractor relationship clause in the previous chapter. This clause stipulates that there will be a number of the consultant's employees involved in the project and sets forth the legal standards governing that relationship. As indicated earlier, it is not only the statement of the relationship that is important, but it is the fact that the parties to the contract adhere to this distinction.

9. All employees of Consultant engaged in any of the Work performed by TSC hereunder at all times and in all places shall be subject to the sole direction, supervision, and control of Consultant. Consultant shall exercise control over the means and manner in which it and its employees perform the Work requested by TSC hereunder, and in all respects Consultant's relationship and the relationship of all of Consultant's employees to TSC shall be that of an independent contractor.

## Notices

Paragraph 11 of the agreement provides for giving notice under the agreement.

11. Unless TSC shall specify otherwise in writing, notices, statements, and all other matters concerning the Work to be performed hereunder shall be addressed to TSC as follows:

Unless Consultant shall specify otherwise in writing, notices, requests for service, and all other matters concerning the Work to be performed hereunder shall be addressed to Consultant as follows:

Any and all notices or other communications required or permitted by this Agreement or by law to be served on or given to either party hereto by the other party hereto shall be in writing and shall be deemed duly served and given upon actual receipt by the party to whom it is directed.

In many places in the contract, the parties exchange information in writing. Paragraph 11 establishes the specific addresses and persons to whom notice should be given to conform to the contract. Paragraph 11 provides that all notices given in the agreement are to be in writing, a practice that should be followed given the specific problems discussed earlier. The last section of paragraph 11 provides that any notices given under the agreement are considered served on the parties only upon their receipt. The purpose of this clause is to counteract a legal doctrine that can provide that a notice is considered given once it has been mailed. In an agreement conducted on an ongoing basis between the parties, such formalism is not necessary. What is important is that the parties actually receive such communications intended to be received and that they are able to act upon them.

## Equal Employment Opportunity

Paragraph 12 incorporates a statement that the corporation is required to include in all its contracts. This contract incorporates a U.S executive order that all government contractors must in turn require the persons doing business with them to agree not to discriminate.

12. There is incorporated herein by reference, Section 202 of Executive Order 11,246, dated September 24, 1965, as amended, to the general effect that Consultant shall not discriminate against any employee or applicant for employment under this agreement because of race,

color, religion, sex, or national origin, and further that Consultant shall take affirmative action to insure that applicants and employees are treated without regard to their race, color, religion, sex, or national origin.

The kind of nondiscrimination clause to be included in all contracts will vary depending on whether the corporation is subject to a regulation or agreement with a federal or state agency. Even if the corporation is not subject to such a requirement, sound practice dictates that the corporation requires all of the individuals doing business with it not to discriminate. This can be accomplished by deleting the first part of paragraph 12 through the words "to the general effect that." The clause then will have a specific provision that the consultant may not discriminate.

## Termination

Paragraph 13 is a termination clause giving broad powers to either side to the contract. It permits the parties to back out of the agreement at any time, providing that projects then under way are completed. It also permits one party or the other to suspend performance temporarily under the agreement.

13. Notwithstanding any other provision hereof, TSC or Consultant may cancel this agreement upon written notice to the other party, pro-vided, however, Consultant may not terminate any Work requested by TSC and not rejected by the Consultant as provided for in para-graph 1 herein by Consultant prior to Consultant's notice of termi-nation hereunder, unless TSC shall so consent. TSC may, however, direct Consultant to terminate any Work at any time, or TSC may suspend Consultant's performance temporarily hereunder or on a specific project hereunder at any time or from time to time. TSC's only obligation under this paragraph 13 for any such cancellation, cessation, suspension, or redirection of the Work being performed by Consultant shall be the payment to Consultant of the fees and authorized expenses for the Work actually performed.

This clause should not be used in every situation, as it may not be in the interest of either the corporation or the consultant to permit such broad termination or suspension privileges. It is aimed at a contractual relationship covering many facets and specific work assignments. It is not appropriate to a contract between the corporation and consultant to perform a single project of limited scope and done within a limited period of time. In such cases, paragraph 13 should be deleted entirely. The last portion of paragraph 13 provides that if the corporation exercises its power it is only liable to pay for the consultant's actual expenses. This negates the obligation of the corporation to the consultant for lost profits that the consultant might have anticipated in completing the performance of a possible task.

Optional paragraph 13 permits either party to cancel the contract upon written notice to the other. It also provides that the employing corporation may direct the consultant to terminate any work under the contract or to suspend its work from time to time. The clause permitting mutual cancellation is fairly common in most contracts, more common than the unilateral termination clause, paragraph 13 in the master contract. Given the fact that either party can cancel the entire contract, it would be unusual for the consultant to not agree that the corporation can terminate a portion of the consultant's work under the contract. This is exercised only when the consultant's work depends upon other projects that have been halted for one reason or another. In addition, such a clause is probably more appropriate when the consultant is being paid by the project, as failing to perform the contract leaves the parties at a loss in terms of paying the consultant on an interim basis.

13. Notwithstanding any other provision hereof, either party may cancel this Agreement upon written notice to the other party. Upon written notice, however, TSC may direct Consultant to terminate any of the Work at any time, or TSC may suspend temporarily Consultant's performance hereunder at any time or from time to time. TSC's only obligation under this paragraph 13 for any such cancellation, cessation, suspension, or redirection of the Work being performed by Consultant shall be the payment to Consultant of the fee for the Work actually performed.

## Assignability

Paragraph 14 is a contractual provision dealing with the assignability of the agreement.

14. This agreement is personal in nature and is not assignable by either TSC or Consultant. Consultant may subcontract portions of its requested Work or services upon approval of the proposed subcontractor by TSC, provided such approval shall not relieve Consultant of its responsibility under this agreement for the Work.

As discussed in chapter 8, designating the agreement "personal" makes it difficult to secure specific enforcement in the courts, so such a clause should be used with caution. The assignability of the contract is a separate but related matter. Paragraph 14 provides that the agreement is not assignable by either the corporation or the consultant, but permits the consultant to subcontract a portion of its work with the approval of the employing corporation. In a large, complex project, such a clause may be desired. If the parties do not want the performance of an essentially simple project to be assigned, however, there seems to be little justification for permitting subcontracting. Of course, the quality of work of the subcontractor and its performance is the responsibility of the consultant; the fact that the corporation has approved the particular subcontractor does not relieve the consultant from its liability for failure to perform.

Optional paragraph 14(a) makes the contract nonassignable but does permit subcontracting.

14. (a) This Agreement is personal in nature and is not assignable by either Consultant or TSC. Consultant may, however, subcontract its services, in whole or in part, to others without the prior approval of TSC. Consultant hereby guarantees to TSC compliance by such other persons with the responsibilities and liabilities herein assumed by Consultant, provided that the limitations on Consultant's liability set forth in the Agreement constitute the aggregate limit of liability of Consultant and its subcontractors to TSC and TSC agrees to hold only Consultant responsible for any failure to so comply. Consultant agrees that TSC will incur no duplication of costs as a result of any such subcontract.

In this clause, the consultant guarantees that the subcontracted performance will comply with the agreement. Optional paragraph 14(a) is designed to fit with optional paragraph 10 in that it expands the limitation of the consultant's liability to include the aggregate liability of the consultant and its subcontractors. Paragraph 14(a) provides that the consultant will assure that there is no duplication of costs as a result of its subcontracting activities.

Optional paragraph 14 provides that either party may assign its rights or delegate its duties with the prior written approval of the other party.

> 14. Either party may assign its rights or delegate its duties under this Agreement with the prior written approval of the other party, provided, however, that such approval shall not relieve Consultant of its responsibility under the Agreement for the Work. Consultant may subcontract portions of the Work without the prior approval of TSC, provided, however, that such subcontracting shall not relieve Consultant of its responsibility under this Agreement for the Work.

This paragraph gives each party substantially more flexibility and may recognize more complex corporate relationships than original paragraph 14. For example, the corporation hiring the consultant may not be the subsidiary for which the services actually are performed. Similarly, the corporation that signs the contract may not be the particular subsidiary in a consulting firm that does the actual work. The contract protects the signing parties by saying that subcontracting responsibilities under the agreement do not change the liability of either party for adequate performance, both for the work under the contract and the payment of bills.

## Subcontractors and Employers

Paragraph 15 should be included when the employing corporation anticipates that others besides an individual consultant are involved. Paragraph 15 binds those persons working for the consultant on this project, in whatever capacity, to certain protective provisions in this agreement, including the ownership of copyrightable products and the retention and delivery of manuscripts and related documents.

> 15. Consultant, its employees, and others whose services may be procured by Consultant to assist Consultant in the performance of the Work shall agree to be bound by the terms of paragraphs 5, 6, 7, 8, and 14 herein, unless waived in writing by TSC.

If the contract is between an individual consultant and a corporation, paragraph 15 is not required, as the individual consultant already has agreed to be bound by all of these provisions. Paragraph 15 permits the employing corporation to waive some of these, in particular where the delivery of a work product from a subcontractor to the consultant and then from the consultant to the corporation adds nothing to the performance of the project but merely necessitates additional expenses.

## Corporate Opportunities and Conflicts of Interest

Paragraph 16 is designed to cover the special relationship between the consultant and the corporation during the term of the agreement.

> 16. During the term of this Agreement, Consultant shall reveal promptly to TSC all matters coming to its attention pertaining to the business of TSC and shall not accept similar employment from, or serve in a similar capacity with, any other concern that is at such time engaged in a business of a like or similar nature to the business now conducted by TSC.

It covers two specific matters. First, it requires that the consultant bring to the corporation's attention all matters pertaining to the corporation's business during the term of this contract. This covers so-called "corporate opportunities." Corporate opportunities include information that the consultant has discovered while engaged on the work of the corporation that will benefit the corporation. The second matter covered in the clause deals with conflict of interest. Under this clause, the consultant may not accept similar employment from another concern engaged in a similar business during the term of the agreement. This is not the same as a "non-compete" clause, which binds the consultant after the term of the contract. As indicated in chapter 8, noncompete clauses are difficult to enforce and should be used only in the most extreme circumstances. If it is desirable to use a non-compete clause, it should be limited both in term and scope. An enforceable non-compete clause will provide that for a term of two years the consultant agrees not to accept similar employment from any other concern engaged in a business directly competitive to the business conducted by the corporation. Anything broader than this may not be able to be enforced at all.

**Insurance**

Paragraph 18 characterizes the schizophrenic attitude of lawyers toward the relationship. After lawyers have established carefully that a relationship cannot be that of an employer and employee and have advised their clients that if the clients meet all the specifications their relationship always will be regarded as that of corporation and independent contractor, they then advise the parties to take all steps to protect themselves in case this should fail. Paragraph 18 is one of these steps.

> 18. Consultant will take out and maintain all insurance required by any governmental unit to meet any statutory requirement and to protect Consultant and TSC fully from and against any and all claims arising out of the Work performed hereunder. Consultant will supply TSC with satisfactory evidence thereof. The cost of such insurance shall not be deemed an authorized expense for the Work.

Essentially, paragraph 18 is aimed at assuring the employer that the consultant has insurance coverage , such as worker's compensation, which the employing corporation is responsible to obtain if the ultimate relationship between the parties is not that of independent contractor and retaining corporation. In a project involving large numbers of employees scattered over wide areas, such a clause is worthwhile. In a project requiring the dedication of limited numbers of personnel in an office, as distinguished from a manufacturing plant, this clause is probably redundant.

Optional paragraph 18 also deals with the question of insurance. In this situation, however, the consultant's expenses in complying with this demand are charged back to the corporation.

> 18. Consultant will take out and maintain all insurance required by any governmental unit to meet any statutory requirement, to protect Consultant and TSC fully from and against any and all claims arising out of the Work performed hereunder, and as requested by TSC. Consultant will supply TSC with satisfactory evidence thereof. The cost of such insurance shall be deemed a Recoverable Cost of the Work as set forth in Exhibit B attached hereto.

## Applicable Law

Paragraph 19 provides that the agreement is governed by the laws of a particular state. This is of particular importance when clauses such as paragraph 18, which key to local law, are included.

19. This Agreement shall be governed by and construed in accordance with the laws of the State of _____.

Generally, a contract is governed by the law of the place where it is made or the law of the place where it is performed. Most contracts will be made and performed in the same place, and a clause such as 19 therefore is not necessary. Clause 19 is required when the parties are aware that performance occurs in several places or the parties do not know where the consultant will be doing the work for the corporation. Clause 19 also is important if some or all of the performance takes place overseas or out of the jurisdiction of the United States. The parties should stipulate some jurisdiction that has a reasonable relationship to the contract, probably the state in which most of the work will be done or the state in which the corporation is located.

## Disputes; Arbitration

Paragraph 20 is one way of handling disputes. It is designed to deal with a situation in which the performance of the consultant may be in several different areas; if there is a dispute, the parties do not know to which court they may proceed. A clause agreeing that courts in a particular state have jurisdiction over the case generally will be honored if that state has some reasonable relationship to the performance of the contract.

20. The United States District Court for the _____ District of _____ shall have jurisdiction with respect to all matters hereunder, and Consultant and TSC hereby submit themselves to the jurisdiction of the United States District Court for the _____ District of _____ for all purposes; provided, however, if the said court shall lack jurisdiction, the (_____ State) Court shall have jurisdiction with respect to all matters hereunder and the parties hereby submit themselves to the jurisdiction of the (_____ State) Court for all purposes.

Paragraph 20 also covers the possibility that a U.S. District Court will not accept jurisdiction, as it does not accept all lawsuits between all parties. It is limited by statute and constitution as to what cases it can take. A major limitation is that the court will not accept a case being fought between two persons it deems residing in the same state. The court's concept of residing is substantially broader than the normal concept, in that a corporation can be residing in the state where it is incorporated or where its principal place of business is. Therefore, this clause provides that the state courts have jurisdiction. An alternative approach is to insert an arbitration clause here, of the nature discussed in chapter 8.

### Amendments; Waivers

Paragraph 21 provides that this contract cannot be changed unless it is changed in writing. In accord with the discussion of the importance of the statute of frauds, this is particularly important. Even if this clause were not in the contract, the practice it specifies should be observed by the parties at all times. By placing this paragraph in the contract, the parties are protecting themselves against oral modification of the agreement in uncontrollable ways in the future.

> 21. Any waiver, alteration, or modification of any of the provisions of this Agreement shall not be valid unless in writing and signed by the parties.

Optional paragraph 21(b) states that no waiver by either party of the default of the other waives future defaults.

> 21. (b) No waiver by either party of any defaults of the other party under this Agreement shall operate as a waiver of any future default, whether of a like or different character.

This paragraph is designed to counteract a legal doctrine stating that if one party permits the other to deviate from the contract without either changing the contract or objecting to the deviation, then this establishes a form of commercial practice between the parties. The doctrine effectively allows the party that has deviated once from the contract to continue to do so without risking being accused of breach of contract. Such an event is most unlikely except in the most complex and far-reaching form of agreement. Where many different individuals are involved in the performance of the work either on the corporation's or the consultant's side, paragraph 21(b) should be considered.

### Integration and Severability Clauses

Paragraph 22 contains what is regarded by lawyers as the integration clause. It is a corollary of the concept that the contract be in writing. It says that the document being signed contains the entire agreement of the parties. This is designed to wipe out any discussions that predate the contract. If the duties are not in the contract, then they do not exist.

> 22. This instrument contains the entire Agreement between TSC and the Consultant, and any agreement or representation respecting the duties of either TSC or the Consultant hereunder not expressly set forth in this instrument is null and void.

Optional paragraph 22(b) provides that if any portion of the contract is held invalid then the entire contract will not fall. This is designed to cover clauses such as liquidated damages, assignments of the right to copyrightable and patentable products, indemnification clauses, and confidentiality and noncompetition clauses, which are the subject of court challenges from time to time. As drafted, the contract reflects the agreement of the parties and does not constitute a one-sided document. Legal doctrines are continually subject to change, however, and if the parties find that one clause of the agreement is unenforceable, the balance of it should stand. Without a clause like this one in an extremely long, complex agreement, the courts in a contract dispute will have to review the entire contract and decide whether the clause under dispute is essential or not. If the clause is deemed essential or critical to the agreement of the parties, the courts will declare the entire contract null and void. To avoid this, clause 22(b) is proposed.

> 22. (b) If any term or provision of this Agreement or the application thereof to any person or circumstance shall, to any extent, be invalid or unenforceable, the remainder of this Agreement, or the application of such term or provision to persons or circumstances other

than those as to which it is held invalid or unenforceable, shall not be affected thereby and each term and provision of this Agreement shall be valid and be enforced to the fullest extent permitted by law.

The closing part of the agreement is the normal conclusion, which provides that both parties will sign the agreement as evidence of their acceptance. As a matter of good practice, each party should receive a signed original of the contract, and care should be taken to see that the signed originals conform precisely with one another. Any variation between two apparent originals can lead to nothing but trouble.

## SPECIALIZED CONTRACTS

Also included in the Appendix are two more specialized documents. The first is a sample of contract language required by the Department of Housing and Urban Development in projects funded through its Community Development Grants program. These are included to illustrate additional ways to handle the same concepts outlined in this and previous chapters. They are not necessarily recommended but are included for illustration. The second is a form of contract for a fund-raising consultant, included to show how the principles elaborated in these chapters can be applied to a specific situation. Fund-raising is an activity subject to increasing question and regulation. Within the past few years, government interest in controlling the way charities dispense money they have collected has increased. For example, in February 1980 a case reached the U.S. Supreme Court where a township ordinance required that a charity demonstrate that at least 75 percent of its receipts were used for charitable purposes in order to be allowed to solicit contributions in the township. The Court decided that a local township could not bar the charity from soliciting funds by imposing such a requirement and declared the ordinance invalid. The sample agreement deals with the issues commonly arising in fund-raising and applies the analysis of the previous chapters to a narrow, specific situation.

# When Things Go Wrong

## WHY DISPUTES ARISE

Although the parties to a consulting agreement may intend never to have a dispute and in fact may expect that their contract covers every possible question that could arise between them, disputes are nevertheless inevitable. The parties to a consulting agreement may differ as to their particular rights or obligations under the agreement, no matter how carefully the document is written and no matter how detailed the specifications of the performance required by each side. These disputes may lead to delays in performance and complaints about the quality of the consultant's work. They may arise out of contentions that the corporation retaining the consultant has not coöperated with the consultant, thereby making his or her job more difficult, or similar operational misunderstandings. It is an unfortunate fact that even with the best of intentions, parties to an agreement may deliver less than they have promised in writing.

## HOW TO HANDLE A DISPUTE

When the parties to a consulting agreement face a dispute, the first question is whether the agreement already covers the subject of the dispute. If the parties have thought through the relationship thoroughly, it is likely their agreement has some provision dealing with the subject of the dispute. If so, the consultant and the corporation should be able to arrive at an amicable conclusion.

A dispute may have to be settled by negotiation when a contract requires some evidence of good faith. If the contract states that the performance of a consultant must be satisfactory to the corporation and the corporation's determination of whether the work product is satisfactory must be made in good faith, the fact that the contract covers the subject may not resolve it. The courts have held that the existence of good faith necessitates an examination not only of the parties' own statements but also of how they behave. This means that such a clause requires both good faith and a demonstration of good faith. For example, if a corporation asserts it cannot use a report, and does not in fact use it, a court will probably find the corporation acted in good faith, even if the consultant can show that some other corporation could use it. But if the court finds that officers of the corporation were concerned about the high cost of the contract (even if the cost is as originally estimated) and then rejected the report, it will probably find the corporation acted in bad faith. Of course, good faith is in the eye of the beholder; a demonstration of good faith can still result in a breakdown in negotiations and ultimately in charges of breach of contract.

Whether the injured party is a corporation or a consultant, before seeking to use the remedies available—that is, suits for breach of contract, specific performance, rescission, restitution, enforcement or liquidated damages clauses, or resort to arbitration or mediation—there are several key steps to follow. The first is that any party that feels it has been damaged by the other party should reread the contract, any amendments made to it, and any instructions that were exchanged between the parties. There are a surprising number of disputes that arise in the commercial world between parties who have not taken this first step to see whether the agreement they have signed covers the disputed points. If the agreement does not cover the dispute, then the parties should look to the practice that has grown up between them in their relationship, for the courts often will look to common commercial practice to determine the rights of the parties. This practice is evidenced by the conduct between the parties to a contract or by what is commonly accepted in similar commercial relationships.

These establish the standards against which any possible breach of contract should be measured. If a party to an agreement believes there has been a breach of contract, it should begin immediately to document that breach and any damages it is suffering, including delays, difficulties in obtaining replacement services, default upon related contracts, and other impacts on its own customers and suppliers. For example, a consulting agreement tied to a particular project can result in various kinds of harm to the parties. If the contract is breached by the corporation, the consultant may find that a source of income has been cut off if the consultant did not enter into another commercial relationship because it was bound for a time to the first. On the other hand, the corporation that believes it has suffered a breach of contract may find that the project for which it has hired the consultant is now in jeopardy. In either case, careful documentation should be the rule.

Communication between the parties in the case of a possible breach of contract should be done carefully. To the greatest extent possible, communication should be in writing to make sure there is a clear understanding between the parties regarding the grievance. The parties already should have made sure that their communications relating to the contract have been reduced to writing to date. Written communication not only protects the parties from violating the statute of frauds, as mentioned before, but protects their positions in the face of possible disputes over the contracts. Although writing can be ambiguous, a written record is substantially easier to review than the incomplete recollection of the parties after a falling out.

## WHAT YOU CAN SUE FOR

When one party suffers a breach of contract, the only legal remedy most people think of is a lawsuit for money damages. In fact, the remedies available to the parties to a consulting contract are varied. Each remedy has its special benefits but also suffers from some limitations. Those most often used in disputes arising out of service contracts are the equitable remedies, a reference to the historical origins in which remedies that did not involve the transfer of money were granted by a court of equity rather than a court of law. These are a lawsuit for breach of contract, an action for restitution, or an action for specific performance. Other remedies available that may involve going to court include rescission, suits for liquidated damages, or arbitration.

### Damages

The basic legal doctrine surrounding breach of contract says that if one party breaches an agreement, the other party may collect the damages necessary to put them in the same position they would have been in had the contract been performed. The problem with the consulting relationship, from the point of view of the corporation, is that since it is purchasing the expertise and services of a consultant often to solve an unknown problem or to come up with new concepts, it has no idea of the value of the work if it was not received. This means that the corporation may not be able to sue for breach of contract because it cannot show how it has been damaged. If there has been a breach of contract, the consultant may face a similar problem, that is, how has the consultant been damaged? If the consultant is to be paid a fixed fee, then clearly the fixed fee can be a measure of damages. If the consultant is to be paid on an hourly basis or on a percentage of money saved, then the damages may be too speculative to award.

This means that the parties may have a right to sue but may not be able to prove collectible damages.

## Restitution

The remedy of restitution is a variation of damages with a different legal tradition. In restitution the courts try to restore to each party the monies expended and attempt to exchange additional money to compensate the parties for expenses incurred. The effort here is to dissolve the contract rather than enforce it and to restore parties to their original positions. Related to this are remedies, usually called equitable remedies, in which the parties to a broken contract sue for value. The consultant sues the corporation to collect the value of his services to the corporation. An alternative is to sue for the value of the services rendered by the consultant in terms of lost time, in the case of the consultant who bills by the hour. There can be a significant difference between the value of the services rendered from the point of view of the consultant and the point of view of the client corporation. The rules regarding which remedy is available attempt to reach the fairest and most equitable solution to a disputed agreement. From the point of view of the corporation, the same choice of remedies exists, that is, to achieve a return of monies expended or some return of value.

## Rescission

Rescission of an agreement is an effort to eliminate the agreement in law and return the parties to a state they would have occupied if the agreement had never existed. The parties wash their hands of the whole affair and are set back to the position they occupied before the contract. In many cases rescission may yield a result similar to restitution, particularly when the case involves the purchase and sale of goods.

In the case of contracts where services are exchanged for money, rescission is a more difficult remedy to obtain from the courts, as there is no real physical commodity to transfer and return. For example, rescission easily can be obtained in the sale of a car; the court can force one party to return the car and the other to return the money. In the case of services, although one party can return the money the services themselves cannot be returned. It is very hard, if not impossible, for a court to force a party to disgorge the benefits of services completely, for once they have been rendered they can never be returned.

## Specific Performance

In the case of a services contract, the most frequent remedy an injured party can seek is specific performance. This means that one party sues the other and asks an intervening court to force the defending party to live up to the terms of the contract. If the corporation is being sued by the consultant, the corporation is forced to coöperate with the consultant in the performance of the consultant's services, to pay the consultant under the terms and conditions agreed upon, and generally restore relations as if they had never broken down. If the corporation is suing the consultant, the court orders the consultant to perform the services promised in the contract under the same standards of care, good faith, and timeliness.

Reference was made earlier to the question of personal services. When a contract with a consultant requires the services rendered to be those of one or more specifically designated individuals, the contract can be regarded as one for personal services. This is an old notion in which the party seeking performance—that is the corporation—enters into a contract with the consultant only on the condition that all the services are performed by an individual who, presumably, possesses unique skills. The more unusual the skills, the more difficult it is for the court to secure performance. The courts generally have held this to be a personal services contract; the performance or work promised under the agreement is always personal and never is able to be delegated. In the past, many courts refused to enforce personal services contracts because they have no way to assure adequate compliance. The courts reasoned that any way a court has at its disposal to force a person to perform, including monetary penalties and the threat of prison, would take away the "spirit" of the performance. The oldest cases go back to the owners of theaters who wished opera singers to honor their contracts and appear. The courts said that the parties clearly had intended an opera singer to perform in a skillful, professional manner, the courts were unable to enforce this agreement, as they had no way to judge the quality of the performance, and even if they had, they had no way acceptable in modern society to insist that the performance be done and be done properly. The courts would not get involved in whether the service was adequate.

After a number of years, the courts arrived at a compromise between the interests of the parties to such an agreement, in this case the corporation and the consultant. In situations where the services are regarded as personal and unique, the courts have continued to hold that they cannot force a person of high skills to perform under such a contract. Under the proper circumstances, however, the courts can keep such a skilled individual from entering into a contract to perform the same services for another person, usually a competitor. The courts feel that if a skilled professional, here the consultant, wishes to refrain from performing special services, they cannot prevent him or her from doing so. But they can prevent him or her from breaching an agreement with the corporation by working for another person and performing the same services. The courts have noted slyly that if the effect of this order is to bring the two disputing parties together again, then they are all for it; this is not their intent, however.

Given the limits on specific performance, the parties should be extremely careful when specifying that the corporation insists that the services being performed under the contract be those of one individual only. It is clear today that the specific performance of a commercial agreement will not be prevented by the courts solely on the grounds that the performance requires the personal involvement of the defendant, but the courts are still reluctant to interfere and to supervise the day-to-day performance of highly skilled and talented individuals.

## MEDIATION

Mediation is not generally regarded as a true remedy in breach of contract. Mediation is bringing in another party to attempt to bridge the differences between the parties and work out an amicable settlement. It is not the same as arbitration, as the recommendations of the mediator are not binding. It gives the parties a chance to review their cases and communicate their differences to a third party who has not participated in the transaction and who, it is hoped, can bring a more detached point of view. If the parties use a mediator properly, they may find they can solve their problems by entering into a new or amended agreement covering the problem that has arisen, settling the dispute it has engendered, and perhaps making some adjustment in the terms of compensation or performance.

A mediator should be someone trusted by each party but whom one party will not feel is aligned too closely with the other. A potential source of mediators or a forum for mediation is the professional organizations discussed in chapter 2. As noted there, although many of these organizations cannot discipline their members formally, they do make available to their members, and in some cases to outside concerns, a place where disputes can be aired. In fact, using these organizations can be productive, as it permits each party to a dispute to make his case and air his grievances without souring what may be an important commercial relationship by resorting to more formal procedures.

## REMEDIES PROVIDED BY AGREEMENT

In the agreement, the parties can handle anticipated disputes in two ways. They can insert a liquidated damages clause, one that provides a kind of penalty for specific breaches of contract, or they can provide that any unresolved disputes will go to arbitration to be resolved.

### Liquidated Damages

One way to handle the performance of unique services by the consultant, or the provision of unique support services by the corporation, is to insert in the contract a liquidated damage clause, which states that if a party breaches a contract, it agrees to pay a set amount of damages to the other party. The original purpose of these clauses was to meet the problem in the breach-of-contract cases above, where the courts were unable to decide how much a party had been injured by the breach by another party to the contract. Liquidated damage clauses often spawn more litigation than they prevent, however. After liquidated damage clauses were accepted, some parties to commercial agreements went to the extreme and inserted liquidated damage clauses of high amounts to prevent the party from breaching the contract with the threat of an onerous fine. The courts decided not to enforce what they regard as penalty clauses but only true liquidated damage clauses. In general, this means that the courts will seek to determine whether, at the signing of the contract, the damages agreed upon were reasonably related to the foreseeable losses that could be incurred by the parties to the contract. They would reject enforcing damage clauses that were so high they constituted a penalty or direct threat to the livelihood of one of the parties to the contract. In practice, this means that the parties must review the major potential breaches of contract in advance and assign a dollar value to them at the beginning of the contract. Not only is this extremely difficult, but it is an unusual subject to inject into the negotiations. The parties who have negotiated in good faith to arrive at a workable agreement also must sit down and decide the most likely ways either or both of them may break that contract and what value they should attach to each of those potential breaches. The net result is that these clauses are few and far between. They are more common in commercial agreements where commodities or financial options are involved, that is, the parties can see that money will be at stake and make an estimate in good faith of potential losses at the beginning of the contract. These good-faith estimates generally are upheld. The courts are reluctant to uphold a personal-services agreement, and therefore a consulting agreement, for some of the same reasons given in the older specific performance cases; that is, the courts will not participate in what they see as coercion through contracts. Some courts have stated this to mean that they will not engage in violations of the constitutional amendment against slavery by forcing people to perform contracts against their will. This overstates the law but should clearly indicate to the parties that there are limits to the use of such penalties as liquidated damage clauses.

## Arbitration

A final option available is to arrange that any disputes are submitted to arbitration. Arbitration is a proceeding in which disputes are submitted for decision by a panel of individuals instead of by a judge. Generally, arbitration occurs in two situations: the parties to a contract agree in the contract to submit any future disputes to arbitration or the parties involved in a current dispute agree to avoid a lawsuit and submit the dispute to arbitration. The kinds of disputes that can go to arbitration are limited only by the terms of the arbitration agreement.

If the parties to a consulting agreement have inserted an arbitration clause, it is more than likely they will use the offices of the American Arbitration Association (AAA) to carry forward the arbitration, although this is not necessary. Some contract clauses specifically provide for arbitration by the AAA under its rules. If the parties wish to provide for this in advance, they should use the arbitration clause provided in the Appendix.

## WHY ARBITRATION IS USED

Controversies arising out of consulting agreements seldom involve major legal issues but usually concern evaluation of facts and interpretation of contract terms. Consequently, when differences arise out of day-to-day commercial relations, parties often prefer to settle them privately and informally in a businesslike manner that encourages continued relationships. That is why many businesses use commercial arbitration.

Arbitration has been used increasingly in recent years for several reasons. First, crowded court calendars make it profitable to resolve disputes without resorting to the judicial process. Second, the AAA has undertaken major efforts to educate business people about arbitration's benefits and effectiveness. Third, it often makes sense to use arbitration instead of the courts to provide a quick decision by experts in the area in dispute. Finally, over three-fourths of the states have enacted specific laws recognizing arbitration by upholding arbitration agreements as valid and enforceable, whether the agreements were entered into before or at the time a dispute arose.

Parties also may provide by special agreement that, so long as the parties have fulfilled its terms, the results of arbitration and its award will be kept confidential. Unless the parties provide otherwise, arbitration proceedings are held in private and are not a matter of public record. Thus, arbitration of disputes provides an additional level of flexibility, particularly where the parties may be disclosing sensitive commercial or business information they do not wish to be made public.

## HOW ARBITRATION WORKS

As arbitration is widely accepted and a remedy agreed upon contractually, it will be discussed at some length. For the purposes of this discussion, the rules and procedures of the AAA's Commercial Arbitration Tribunal will be examined to show the general manner in which arbitration works. The AAA is selected as a model as it administers a large portion of all commercial arbitrations. Arbitration is available in other ways, and most states have adopted a uniform arbitration act that permits parties to agree to arbitration for virtually all disputes. Some states also have given various courts the power to permit arbitration under other auspices. In cases where arbitration is not conducted by the AAA, the parties may have to adopt particular rules pertaining to their dispute and how it will be handled in arbitration. For that reason many parties anticipating disputes not of major financial significance simply will refer all disputes to the AAA in advance. The arbitration services of the AAA are available to both members and nonmembers. (For convenience, a list of regional offices through which AAA arbitration is administered is included in the Appendix.)

The first step in initiating arbitration is to see that there is an agreement to arbitrate. This agreement may be one of two kinds: a future-dispute arbitration clause in a contract, or when the parties did not provide in advance for arbitration, an agreement to submit existing disputes to arbitration. Included in the Appendix is a copy of the AAA's demand-for-arbitration form, based upon a typical contract clause to submit all future disputes to arbitration. Also in the Appendix is a form of submission agreement, prepared as a model by the AAA. This agreement shows how parties to a contract that does not include an arbitration clause may nonetheless agree, after the dispute has arisen, to submit their dispute to arbitration under the AAA rules. The AAA supplies these forms on request free of charge.

Regardless of the form of the agreement to arbitrate, notification to AAA and the defending party of the claim is all that is required to begin arbitration. On receiving the initiating papers, the AAA assigns to the case one of its staff members, the tribunal administrator, who handles administration and assists both sides in all procedural matters until the award is made. The AAA charges an administrative fee based upon the amount of each claim and counterclaim. The fee is due and payable at the time of filing. Unless the parties agree otherwise, the fee is paid by both of them under the AAA rules. Unless the parties have indicated another method, the AAA follows a basic system for selecting the arbitrator. On receiving the demand for arbitration or submission agreement, the tribunal administrator sends each party a copy of the same list of proposed arbitrators technically qualified to resolve the dispute. In drawing up the list, the tribunal administrator is guided by the nature of the dispute. Parties are allowed seven days to review the list, cross out any names they object to, and number the remaining names in order of preference. When parties want more information about a proposed arbitrator, such information is gladly given on request. These lists are then returned to the AAA. The tribunal administrator compares indicated preferences and notes the mutual choices. When parties are unable to find a mutual choice from the list, additional lists may be submitted at the request of both parties. If the parties cannot agree on an arbitrator, the AAA will make an administrative appointment; in no case will an arbitrator whose name was crossed out by either party be appointed. Under some arbitration clauses, each party to a dispute appoints one arbitrator, and the two select a third arbitrator from AAA panels in accordance with the procedures described above. To avoid the danger that a compromise award may have to be rendered for the sake of a majority, the parties sometimes provide, and the AAA recommends, that the third arbitrator be permitted to render the award alone when a unanimous award is not possible. This may be done by the parties in their agreement to arbitrate or in a later written stipulation.

Arbitration hearings are somewhat like court trials, except they are less formal. Arbitrators are not required to follow strict rules of evidence; they hear all the evidence material to the issue but determine for themselves what is relevant. Arbitrators therefore are permitted to accept evidence that may not be allowed by judges. The complaining party usually proceeds first with its case. This order may be changed if the arbitrator thinks it necessary. In any event, the burden of proof is not on one side more than the other. Each party tries to convince the arbitrator of the correctness of its position, and no hearing is closed until both have had an opportunity to do so. After both sides have presented all their evidence, the arbitrator closes the hearing. The arbitrator then has thirty days to render an award, unless the arbitration agreement provides otherwise. The award is the decision of the arbitrator upon the matters submitted under the arbitration agreement. If the arbitration board consists of more than one arbitrator, the majority decision is binding. The award is made to dispose of the dispute. It is made within the limits of the arbitration agreement, and the arbitrator must rule on each claim submitted. Once an arbitration award is made, either party can ask a court to confirm the award. Confirmation means that the arbitration award has the same effect as any court decision and can be enforced just as any judgment can.

# APPENDIX

(Note: All blanks are to be completed by inserting the titles of officers, the names of divisions of the corporation, or other appropriate information.)

## SAMPLE CORPORATE POLICY

*Subject:* Outside Consultants

*Summary:* Establishes policies to be followed by all Divisions in determining when to use outside consultants.

*Definition:* Outside consultants provide those personal and professional services of a purely advisory nature, such as the development of policy. They do not perform operating functions or supervise those functions. Outside consultants' services include advice about management and administration; these services do not include commercial and industrial services or research. The services of outside consultants are provided by persons and firms generally considered to have expertise, knowledge, and ability of particular value to a Division.

*Policy:*
1. Each Division issues procedures, to be approved by _____, which require that:
   a. every requirement for outside consultants be justified in writing;
   b. agreements with outside consultants be complete and specify a fixed period of performance for the services to be provided; and
   c. legal and budget review of all agreements for services in excess of one year or costing over $5,000.00 be obtained.
2. Outside consultants may be used by Divisions when:
   a. specialized opinions or professional or technical advice is required and is not available with the Corporation;
   b. an outside point of view on a critical issue is necessary;
   c. state-of-the-art knowledge, education, or research is needed;
   d. opinion(s) of noted experts with national or international prestige is essential to the success of a key project; or
   e. services of special personnel who are not needed full time or cannot serve full time are required.
3. Each Division establishes specific levels of delegations of authority to approve the use of outside consultants. At least _____ levels of approval are required to hire an outside consultant.

*Comments:* There are many situations in which the use of outside consultants are appropriate and necessary. Repeated or extended arrangements should be avoided. Outside consultants are not permitted to make policy or management decisions and should never be used to bypass or undermine personnel limits. Whenever possible, corporate personnel should be utilized to perform the tasks set forth above.

### Additional Policy Provisions on Outside Consultants

1. Any outside consultant must agree, in writing, to be bound by the corporation's policies.
2. A copy of the final report of each outside consultant, or a summary of the services performed if no final report is prepared, will be forwarded to _____ upon completion of the assignment.
3. The Executive in charge of the assignment will prepare a Consultant Appraisal and Review Form at the conclusion of an assignment and forward it to _____.
4. Prior to retaining any outside consultant, the Executive in charge of the assignment will:
   a. ascertain that the same or substantially similar work has not been done or is not now being done elsewhere in the corporation by contacting _____; and
   b. obtain from _____ an appraisal of the consultant under consideration and recommendations of other firms capable of carrying out the assignment, based upon a corporate appraisal previously submitted, internal recommendations, outside references, interviews, and other searches for competent consultants not previously used by the corporation.
5. Upon retaining an outside consultant, the Executive in charge of the assignment will complete a Consultant Retention Form and forward it to _____.
6. Each Division, in its annual budget, must include a detailed description of the nature and projected cost of any consulting work being requested as well as the names of the consultants being considered.
7. Any outside consulting needed after the annual budget has been approved and not detailed in that budget must be approved by _____ if the estimated annual cost of the contract will exceed $_____.

## FEDERAL DEFINITIONS

*Office of Personnel Management:* "Consultant means a person who serves as an adviser to an officer or instrumentality of the Government, as distinguished from an officer or employee who carries out the agency's duties and responsibilities. He gives his views or opinions on problems or questions presented him by the agency, but he neither performs nor supervises performance of operating functions. Ordinarily, he is expert in the field in which he advises, but he need not be a specialist. His expertness may consist of a high order of broad administrative, professional, or technical experience indicating that his ability and knowledge make his advice distinctively valuable to the agency."

*Department of Transportation:* "The term 'consultants' means those persons whose advice and counsel are sought on matters of Departmental interest."

*Department of Energy:* "Consultant awards provide those services of a purely advisory nature relating to the governmental functions of agency administration and management and agency program management. These services are normally provided by persons and / or organizations who are generally considered to have knowledge and special abilities that are not generally available within the agency. The form of compensation is irrelevant."

*Department of Health and Human Services:* "Consultant services are those services which are intended to assist, advise, or render an option and are performed by individuals, firms, or institutions which have exceptional qualifications of skill, experience, or education. Such services include examination, survey, study, analysis, review, evaluation of effectiveness, efficiency, or economy of organizations, management systems, processes, performance standards, procedures, space or equipment layout, programs, or program operations."

*U.S. Senate Committee on Governmental Affairs, Subcommittee on Reports, Accounting, and Management:* "Consultant means a person who serves as an adviser to an officer or instrumentality of the Government, as distinguished from an officer or employee who carries out the agency's duties and responsibilities. He gives his views or opinions on problems or questions presented him by the agency, but he neither performs nor supervises performance of operating functions."

## OFFICE OF MANAGEMENT AND BUDGET CIRCULAR A-120

### Guidelines for the Use of Consulting Services

1. *Purpose.* The Circular establishes policy and guidelines to be followed by executive branch agencies in determining and controlling the appropriate use of consulting services obtained from individuals and organizations. This Circular supersedes OMB Bulletin No. 78-11, dated May 5, 1978, on the same subject.

2. *Background.* OMB Bulletin No. 78-11 was based largely upon data received from the agencies in response to the President's memorandum of May 12, 1977, which asked the heads of agencies to assure that consulting service arrangements of their organizations were both appropriate and necessary. The Bulletin was issued to meet the identified need for uniformity of definition, criteria, and management controls among the agencies.

   This Circular provides permanent guidance in lieu of the interim guidance provided by the Bulletin. To assist agencies in identifying consulting services, as defined in the Bulletin and this Circular, an expanded list of examples is included in the Attachment to this Circular.

   An additional policy is provided in this Circular with respect to responsibility for final determination of whether or not a proposed procurement action is for consulting services, as defined in this Circular.

3. *Relationship to OMB Circular No. A-76.* In summary, OMB Circular No. A-76, "Policies for Acquiring Commercial or Industrial Products and Services Needed by the Government" revised March 29, 1979, directs that:

   Governmental functions must be performed by Government employees (reference 4b and 5f of A-76);

   Commercial or industrial products and services should be provided in the most economical manner through the use of rigorous cost comparisons of private sector and Government performance (reference 4c of A-76); and

   Consulting services are not either of the above categories and should be provided either by Government staff organizations or from private sources, as deemed appropriate by executive agencies in accordance with executive branch guidance on the use of consulting services (reference 6d(5) of A-76).

4. *Coverage.* The provisions of this Circular apply to consulting services

obtained by the following arrangements:

a. Personnel appointment;

b. Procurement contract; and

c. Advisory committee membership.

5. *Definition.* As used for administrative direction in this Circular, *Consulting Services* means those services of a purely advisory nature relating to the governmental functions of agency administration and management and agency program management. (See Attachment for examples of the type of services to which this Circular applies.)

These services are normally provided by persons and / or organizations who are generally considered to have knowledge and special abilities that are not generally available within the agency. The form of compensation is irrelevant to the definition.

6. *Basic Policy*

a. Consulting services will not be used in performing work of a policy / decision making or managerial nature which is the direct responsibility of agency officials.

b. Consulting services will normally be obtained only on an intermittent or temporary basis; repeated or extended arrangements are not to be entered into except under extraordinary circumstances.

c. Consulting services will not be used to bypass or undermine personnel ceilings, pay limitations, or competitive employment procedures.

d. Former Government employees per se will not be given preference in consulting service arrangements.

e. Consulting services will not be used under any circumstances to specifically aid in influencing or enacting legislation.

f. Grants and cooperative agreements will not be used as legal instruments for consulting service arrangements.

g. The contracting officer shall be responsible for determining whether a requested solicitation or procurement action, regardless of dollar value, is for consulting services. The contracting officer's determination shall be final. Prior to processing any solicitation or procurement action for consulting services, the contracting officer shall insure that the applicable provisions of this Circular have been adhered to and that documentation required by the Circular (see 8.a. and 8.b.) is complete and included in the official contract file. The contracting officer will also insure that awards over $10,000 are identified as consulting service contracts on either the agency's data collection form (which conforms to the requirements of the Federal Procurement Data System) or optional Form 279, for input into the Federal Procurement Data System (reference 9.b.).

7. *Guidelines for use of Consulting Services.* Consulting service arrangements may be used, when essential to the mission of the agency, to:

a. Obtain specialized opinions or professional or technical advice which does not exist or is not available within the agency or another agency.

b. Obtain outside points of view to avoid too limited judgment on critical issues.

c. Obtain advice regarding developments in industry, university, or foundation research.

d. Obtain the opinion of noted experts whose national or international prestige can contribute to the success of important projects.

e. Secure citizen advisory participation in developing or implementing Government programs that, by their nature or by statutory provision, call for such participation.

8. *Management Controls*

a. Each agency will assure that for all consulting service arrangements:

(1) Every requirement is appropriate and fully justified in writing. Such justification will provide a statement of need and will certify that such services do not unnecessarily duplicate any previously performed work or services;

(2) Work statements are specific, complete and specify a fixed period of performance for the service to be provided;

(3) Contracts for consulting services are competitively awarded to the maximum extent practicable to insure that costs are reasonable;

(4) Appropriate disclosure is required of, and warning provisions are given to, the performer(s) to avoid conflict of interest; and

(5) Consulting service arrangements are properly administered and monitored to insure that performance is satisfactory.

b. Each agency will establish specific levels of delegation of authority to approve the need for the use of consulting services, based on the policy and guidelines contained in this Circular. Written approval of all consulting service arrangements will be required at a level above the organization sponsoring the activity. Additionally, written approval for all consulting service arrangements during the fourth fiscal quarter will be required at the second level above the organization sponsoring the activity.

    c. OMB Circular No. A-63, Advisory Committee Management, governs policy and procedures regarding advisory committees and their membership.

    d. The Federal Personnel Manual (FPM), Chapter 304, governs policy and procedures regarding personnel appointments.

    e. Until the Federal Acquisition Regulation is published, the Federal Procurement Regulation and the Defense Acquisition Regulation govern policy and procedures regarding contracts.

9. *Data Requirements.* The following data systems will continue to provide information on consulting service arrangements within the executive branch:

    a. Central Personnel Data File (CPDF), operated by the Office of Personnel Management, will have data on personnel appointments, segregating consultants, experts, and advisory committee members (as defined in OMB Circular No. 63).

    b. Federal Procurement Data System (FPDS) will have data on contract arrangements.

    c. Advisory committee data will continue to be maintained in accordance with OMB Circular No. A-63.

10. *Effective date.* This Circular is effective immediately.

11. *Implementation.* All executive branch agencies have previously implemented OMB Bulletin No. 78-11. That implementation is applicable to this Circular and will continue under the guidance of this Circular.

    To implement the new policy with respect to responsibility for final determination of whether or not a proposed procurement action is for consulting services, the Secretary of Defense and the Administrator for General Services are directed to incorporate the applicable provisions of this Circular (see 6.g.) into the Defense acquisition Regulation and the Federal Procurement Regulations, respectively, within sixty (60) days of the date of this Circular.

12. *Inquiries.* All questions or inquiries should be submitted to the Office of Management and Budget. Telephone Number (202) 395-6810.

 

                                     (signed) James T. McIntyre, Jr.
                                               Director

## Attachment

This attachment contains examples of the type of services which are consulting services, as defined in this Circular, and to which this Circular applies.

Advice on or evaluation of agency administration and management, such as:

Organizational structures;

Reorganization plans;

Management methods;

Zero-base budgeting procedures;

Mail handling procedures;

Records and file organization;

Personnel procedures;

Discriminatory labor practices;

Agency publications;

Internal policies, directives, orders,
manuals, and procedures;
and

Management information systems.

Advice on or evaluation of agency program management, such as:

Program plans;

Acquisition strategies;

Assistance strategies;

Regulations;

Assistance or procurement, solicited or unsolicited technical and cost
proposals;

Legal aspects;

Economic impacts;

Program impact; and

Mission and program analysis.

This Circular also applies to any contract task assignment for consulting services given to Federally Funded Research and Development Centers.

See OMB Circular No. A-76 for examples of Governmental functions and commercial and industrial products and services. It should also be noted that the conduct of research and development and technology assessments are not consulting services.

## CONSULTANT RETENTION FORM

Name and address of consulting firm retained:

_____

_____

Member of firm responsible for this account: _____

Date retained: _____ Retention authorized by: _____

Nature of assignment:

( ) Planning          ( ) Employee          ( ) Taxes
( ) Marketing              relations        ( ) Organizational
( ) Regulatory        ( ) Investments       ( ) Financial
( ) Customer          ( ) Real estate       ( ) Acquisitions
      relations       ( ) Government
                            relations

( ) Other _____

Brief summary of assignment: _____

_____

_____

The consulting firm retained has been given a contract confirming its
retention and specifying the terms and conditions of its assignment.
A copy of it is attached.

_____

(Signed)

## SAMPLE LETTER CONFIRMING RETENTION OF A CONSULTANT

(Addressee)

Dear Sir/Madam:

    We are pleased that you will be able to work with us in connection with the _____ project.

    As we have discussed, I will be involved in this project and will resolve those major issues arising during this project that involve either policy considerations or strategy. If you have any questions regarding which tasks you are to perform or how you are to perform them, I will answer them. In addition, if there are any questions on the manner in which you are to proceed, such as access to confidential company information, I will be responsible for resolving them.

    I am enclosing a copy of the agreement we have previously discussed, setting forth the terms and conditions of your assignment. Please sign one copy and return it to me. Keep the other for your files.

    I have enclosed a copy of our billing procedures, which you will need. Please see that all services performed for us and all statements rendered in connection with those services are prepared in conformance with these procedures.

    We look forward to working with you.

                      Very truly yours,


                      (signed by the Executive in charge of the assignment)


### Consultant Billing Procedures

Except where otherwise agreed to in writing, the Corporation is to be charged for services rendered on its behalf only on the basis of the application of the Firm's standard hourly or daily rate for the categories of employees performing the services. In addition, the Corporation will be charged for services rendered by other consultants, accountants, or experts only when they have been retained directly by the Corporation's Executive in charge of the assignment.

A statement for services rendered may be submitted to the Corporation as frequently as the consultant desires. In any case, a statement must be submitted to the Corporation within 30 days following the end of any month in which the total services and disbursements exceed $_____ , and within 30 days following the end of the calendar quarter. For accounting purposes, a statement through November 30 must be submitted by December 10. A written estimate of the total December statement must be submitted on the first working day each January.

Each statement shall set forth, with respect to each assignment, the following:

1.  The number of hours or days spent by each category of employee of the Firm on the assignment;
2.  The billing rate for each category of employee of the Firm on the assignment;
3.  The total disbursements made to other consultants, accountants, and experts;
4.  All expenses and disbursements;
5.  The total due the Firm for the billing period.

In addition, the statement shall indicate by whom it was prepared, and the period it covers and shall be accompanied by any statements rendered the Firm by other consultants, accountants, and experts.

Although it is assumed that the Corporation Executive in charge of this assignment is fully familiar with the nature of the services performed by the consultant on each assignment during the period covered by the statement, the statement should detail the various services that were performed in connection with the assignment.

## CONSULTANT APPRAISAL AND REVIEW FORM

Name and address of consulting firm retained:

_____

_____

Member of firm responsible for this account:

_____

Date retained: _____ Retention authorized by:_____

Nature of assignment:

( ) Planning      ( ) Employee      ( ) Taxes
( ) Marketing          relations      ( ) Organizational
( ) Regulatory      ( ) Investments      ( ) Financial
( ) Customer      ( ) Real estate      ( ) Acquisitions
     relations      ( ) Government
                       relations

( ) Other_____

Brief summary of assignment:_____

_____

_____

Summary of appraisal and review:

The members of the firm who provided services on this account:

( ) Outstanding      ( ) Good      ( ) Fair      ( ) Poor

Other employees of the firm principally involved on this assignment were:

(Name) _____

( ) Outstanding      ( ) Good      ( ) Fair      ( ) Poor

(Name) _____

( ) Outstanding      ( ) Good      ( ) Fair      ( ) Poor

(Name) _____

( ) Outstanding     ( ) Good     ( ) Fair     ( ) Poor

The overall quality of services provided by the firm on this assignment was:

( ) Outstanding     ( ) Good     ( ) Fair     ( ) Poor

Future recommendations:

The services of this firm should be

( ) Used for more outside work in the following areas:_____

_____

( ) Limited to outside work in the following areas:_____
( ) Not used for any future assignments.

Other comments:

_____

_____

_____


_____

(Signed)

## ALTERNATIVE SAMPLE CORPORATE POLICY

*Policy:* Retention, Payment and Evaluation of Outside Consultants
  I. Introduction
     From time to time, it is necessary or desirable in the conduct of the affairs of the Corporation to retain outside consultants. This policy will set forth procedures for retention, billing, payment, and evaluation of outside consultants.
 II. Retention
     Consultants will be retained only by vice-presidents of the Corporation after obtaining authorization from _____.
     After authorization has been obtained, the Executive in charge shall submit a completed Consultant Retention Form, a specimen of which is set forth as Appendix A. After review, _____ will forward it to _____, who will maintain an outside consultant file by specialty.
III. Billing and Payment
     The Executive in charge of the assignment, at the time of retention, shall send to the consultant retained the Billing Procedures, a copy of which is set forth as Appendix B. It provides that a statement of services may be submitted at such intervals as the Executive in charge of the assignment desires, but in any event, a statement shall be submitted within 30 days following the end of each calendar quarter or within 30 days following any month in which the billed services and expenses exceed _____.
     Upon receiving a statement for services rendered, the Executive in charge of the assignment will review it, and if found acceptable, date and initial the statement and forward it to _____ for final approval. Accounts payable will process for payment only those statements that bear the approval of _____. The check for payment will be disbursed directly by Accounts Payable unless different instructions relative to the disbursement of a check have been given.
 IV. Evaluation
     By the tenth of the month following a calendar quarter and upon receipt of a final bill, a fully completed Consultant Appraisal and Review Form, a specimen of which is attached as Appendix C, shall be submitted to _____.

**DEPARTMENT OF HEALTH AND HUMAN SERVICES POLICY ON
CONSULTANT SERVICES**

Chapter 8-15
Consultant Services

8-15-00 Purpose
    10 Scope
    20 Definition of Consultant Services
    30 Policies
    40 Acquisition and Management of Consultant Services
    50 Contract Modifications
    60 Acquisition and Management of Consultant Services Obtained Through Purchase Order
    70 Implementation

Exhibits
X8-15-1 Consultant Services Exclusions
    2 Consultant Services Budget Instructions
    3 Consultant Services Plan
    4 Request for Consultant Services
    5 Assessment of Consultant Services

*8-15-00 Purpose*
This chapter establishes the policies and procedures applicable to the acquisition, management, and control of consultant services.

*8-15-10 Scope*
  A. The policies apply to consultant services as defined in Section 8-15-20.
  B. Consultant services excluded from the requirements of this Chapter are listed in Exhibit X8-15-1.
  C. Except for the reporting requirements in Exhibits X8-15-2 and 3, the policies do not apply to employment of experts and consultants covered in the Federal Personnel Manual, Chapter 304.

*8-15-20 Definition of Consultant Services*
Consultant services are those services which are intended to assist, advise, or render an opinion and are performed by individuals, firms, or institutions which have exceptional qualifications of skill, experience, or education. Such services include examination, survey, study, analysis, review, evaluation, technical assis-

tance or reporting; and have as their purpose the improvement in or evaluation of effectiveness, efficiency, or economy of organizations, management, systems, processes, performance standards, procedures, space or equipment layout, programs, or program operations.

Consultant services falling under the above definition and to which these policies, criteria, management control processes and reporting requirements apply fall into four broad categories irrespective of whether they are purchased by salary and expenses (S&E) or program funds:

A. Services which support or apply to internal operations of staff offices or operating agencies of the Department. Such services would include, but not be limited to, analysis and evaluation of organizations, planning, management, functions, and processes; technical and training assistance; conference management; data systems development; and development of information materials.

B. Services which are in direct support, or apply to, the planning, management and operations of external organizations funded by the Department. Such services include technical and training assistance; audit and management reviews of program funded organizations; and audits of providers of services.

C. Services in connection with surveys, to include design of survey forms, conduct of survey, data preparation and processing, and data analysis. (Surveys not included under this definition are discussed in Exhibit X8-15-1).

D. Services in performing program evaluation studies. Program evaluation studies are those which seek to formally assess existing federal policies or programs (or their components). Such services are performed to reach conclusions concerning program performance, with respect either to program objectives or other significant intended or unintended effects, in order to assist future policy decisions. Types of evaluations include studies of program impact, effectiveness, efficiency, or strategy, as well as support studies to develop new methodology or to develop data to be used in subsequent evaluations.

The consultant services definition should be interpreted in the broadest sense. Accordingly, unless a service is excluded (see Exhibit X8-15-1) it should be considered a consultant service. Requests with supporting rationale for additional exclusions should be directed to the Assistant Secretary for Management and Budget (ASMB).

*8-15-30 Policies—Conditions Permitting and Excluding the Use of Consultant Contracts*

A. The Department permits the use of consultant services:

when work that must be accomplished is critical to the planning, development, operation or evaluation of a departmental program; where such work cannot be accomplished by agency, HEW or other Federal employees;[1] and the service is normally and economically available from the private sector; or when the work is mandated by law to be performed by a consultant.

B. The Department prohibits the use of consultant services:

when the work is making departmental policy decisions or performing departmental management functions which should be retained directly by agency officials. The Secretary reserves the right to approve the use of consultant services for policy making.

when the consultant arrangement is used as a device to bypass or undermine personnel ceilings, pay limitations, or competitive employment procedures.

when the work is personal services which must be performed by departmental employees.

when a project officer is not available who will have sufficient time for adequate work statement development and monitoring of the project after contract award.

*8-15-40 Acquisition and Management of Consultant Services*
This section prescribes procedures applicable to the acquisition and management of consultant services. The procedures cover the following six areas:

budgeting for consultant services,

requests for consultant services,

certifying requests for contracts,

procurement of consultant services,

administration of consultant service contracts, and

assessing and using deliverable products acquired from consultant services.

The procedures are designed to improve planning and budgeting for consultant services; establish responsibilities for certifying consultant service requests;

---

[1] Other Federal employees are available on a project basis from the National Bureau of Standards, the Federal ADP Simulation Center, the National Archives and Records Service and other like organizations.

assure that contracts are properly managed; assure that products delivered are useful to the Department; and establish reporting requirements for consultant services.

*A. Budgeting for Consultant Services*

During budget preparation and allocation, the program and administrative managers must identify future requirements for consultant services. This process will be done in two stages:

First, managers must develop budget estimates of consultant services by categories as described in Exhibit X8-15-2. Budget estimates will include broad explanations of the need for consultant services. The Assistant Secretary for Management and Budget (ASMB) annually will call for the consultant services budget estimates in December. The consultant service budget estimates will be provided in February to the ASMB. The ASMB will provide the consultant service budget estimates to Congressional Appropriations Committees on March 1. (Note that this is an estimating process that occurs 7 months before the fiscal year begins.)

Second, in March, six months prior to the beginning of the fiscal year, the ASMB will issue instructions for the preparation of the consultant services plan. The Assistant Secretary for Planning and Evaluation (ASPE) will issue additional instructions for the evaluation and survey portions of the plan. The consultant services plan will translate the broad consultant services estimates into a plan that identifies specific projects to be procured. The consultant services plan must conform to approved budget estimates, ceilings, or other limitations imposed by the ASMB, in coordination with the ASPE for evaluation projects. Details for preparing the consultant services plan are in Exhibit X8-15-3.

In September, the plan will be forwarded to the ASMB. The evaluation and survey portions of the plan, which will be forwarded through the ASPE, should be drawn from the Agency Research, Evaluation, and Statistical plan. The ASMB will review the consultant services plan to ensure that POC, OS staff office and regions projects are within expenditure ceilings. After forwarding the consultant services plan, a copy of the plan should be used by the program or administrative offices and the procurement offices to develop the consultant services portion of the fiscal year procurement plan required by the Secretary. Preparation of the consultant services plan should not preclude or interfere with first quarter consultant procurements. Accordingly, program and administrative offices can prepare and certify first quarter RFCs provided the project is included in the POC, OS staff office or regions consultant services plan.

During the fiscal year, the POC or OS staff office head or the Principal Regional Official (PRO) may modify the plan provided he/she reprograms the funds from a previously planned project to the new project. When this occurs the procurement office should be notified and a planned procurement date should be established.

If at any time during the fiscal year, any POC or OS staff office head or PRO expects that he/she will exceed consultant services plan estimate by more than 5 percent, a memorandum should be sent to notify the Deputy Assistant Secretary, Finance.

As stated in the Secretary's May 18, 1977 memorandum on correcting contracting deficiencies, POC and OS staff office heads and PROs will have to report quarterly to the Under Secretary variances from the procurement plan awards schedule and the number and amount of sole source awards.

*B. Requests for Consultant Services*

The program or administrative project officer is responsible for developing and coordinating the request for contract (RFC). When developing the RFC, the project office must consider the seven key points that are listed in Exhibit X8-15-4.

*C. Certifying Requests for Contracts*

The POC head or OS staff office head must certify requests for contracts that are for:

consultant services which are noncompetitive and which are for $25,000 or more,

logistical and substantive support for conferences,

management studies of internal organizations, and development of internal procedures or handbooks, and

development of procedures for implementing departmental policy where the implementation requires only adaption of departmental policies and procedures to the needs of the particular agency.

The POC head or OS staff office head must certify or may delegate to his/her principal deputy the responsibility for certifying competitive RFCs valued at $25,000 or more and noncompetitive RFCs that are between $10,000 and $25,000 provided he/she approves the certification process and provided the certification responsibility is not further delegated. In addition, the Assistant Secretary for Health may delegate the certification responsibility to PHS agency heads and the Assistant Secretary for Education may delegate the responsibility to the Commissioner of Education and to the Director of the National Institute of Education. The individual responsible for certifying RFCs may further delegate the certification responsibility one management level for competitive RFCs that are valued at less than $25,000.

In regions, RFCs that are developed by POC regional offices must be certified by the POC individual responsible for certification. RFCs that are developed by regional staff offices which report directly into the Office of the Secretary, such as the Audit Agency, must be certified by the OS staff office individual responsible for certifications. The PRO certifies the RFCs of offices which report directly to him.

The information necessary for certifying RFCs is included in the consultant services plan discussed in section X8-15-40A. Prior to certifying a RFC the program or administrative project officer must provide to the certifying official information that:

> confirms that the RFC embodies the information that was in the consultant services plan relative to certification, or
>
> is new or different from information previously provided in the consultant services plan and that is relevant to certification, or
>
> is relevant for certification of projects that were not included in the consultant services plan.

The individual certifying the RFC is confirming that information relevant to the following points has been provided and that he/she agrees with the information. Specifically, the individual is confirming that:

> the use of consultant services is not prohibited.
>
> the end results expected of the contract justify the anticipated costs,
>
> the sponsoring office evaluated alternatives to satisfy the work requirements,
>
> the planned utilization of the deliverable products is appropriate,
>
> qualified in-house staff to perform the work are not available,
>
> a like product which could satisfy the requirements of the proposal is not available, and
>
> if for information development, collection, or storage, that the information is not available from other appropriate federal agencies such as the National Technical Information Service.

*D. Procurement of Consultant Services*

Procurement requirements are set forth in Federal and in HEW Procurement Regulations.

While the procurement office has the authority to award a contract, the POC or OS staff office head or, for regional contracts, the PRO must approve the award if the contract is noncompetitive and is to be awarded to an organization employing, on the contract, a recent former professional employee(s) of HEW (within the last two years). To carry out the intent of this requirement, the contracting officer will require the offerors to identify former professional HEW employees to be employed on the contract. The POC head, OS staff office head, or PRO must assure and document that there is no collusion or conflict of interest before approving the award.

The procurement office must report contracts it has awarded to the Department-wide Contracts Information System (DCIS). (See Contract Information System User Manual.)

*E. Administration of Consultant Services Contracts*

The program or administrative project officer and contracting officer are responsible for monitoring contractor performance. To facilitate this process, the contractor will prepare a monthly progress report. The project officer, the contracting officer, and the contractor's representative should conduct periodic meetings to discuss the consultant's progress. (As appropriate, meetings may be conducted by telephone.)

If slippages, nondeliveries, or other problems are discovered, the project officer will assess the impact on the terms of the contract and successful completion of the contract, and advise the contracting officer of the problems and recommended actions. The contracting officer must review the situation and take appropriate action, including withholding of payments, cure notices, or other appropriate termination proceedings per HEW Procurement Manual Circular 77.7 and HEWPR Subpart 3-86.

*F. Assessing and Using Deliverable Products Acquired From Consultant*
  *Services*

During this part of the procurement process, the program or administrative officer assesses and accepts the contract deliverables; the contracting officer closes out the contract; and the deliverable products are used.

To achieve the purpose of a contract, the program or administrative officer must establish criteria on which a deliverable product can be judged. Acceptance criteria for deliverables are normally stated in a description of the deliverable products or in a separate contract section.

The actual acceptance of a deliverable should be based on the contractor satisfying the criteria in the contract as opposed to judging the deliverable on criteria that were not included in the contract. If the contractor fails to deliver acceptable products or otherwise perform under the contract, the contracting officer is responsible to determine, with the advice of the program officer and other appropriate technical, cost, and legal advisers, what recourse is appropriate, and to take that action on behalf of the Government.

For contracts, including contract modifications, costing in excess of $25,-000, part of the contract close out will include preparation of a report by the project officer that assesses products delivered by the contractor (see Exhibit X8-15-5). The assessment involves:

> explaining how the purpose or objectives were or were not achieved. In this regard the program office should explain how well the product satisfied acceptance criteria.

> explaining the impact of the consultant findings or recommendations. In this regard, the program office needs to: (1) describe the use of the products that was anticipated when the request for consultant services was certified; (2) state if the intended use of the product has been modified as a result of the contract; and (3) provide a timetable during which major implementation actions will occur.

After preparing the report, the project officer provides the report to the contracting officer. The contracting officer should retain a copy of the report in the official contract file. In addition, the contracting officer sends a copy of the report through the individual responsible for certifying the requests for contracts to the Deputy Assistant Secretary, Finance (DASF). The DASF provides, quarterly, the assessment reports to Congress.

*8-15-50 Contract Modification*

There are two types of contract modifications, minor and major:

> minor modifications include exercising contract options; modifications which extend product delivery dates or contract completion dates; and cumulative cost of modifications which do not increase the contract cost by $25,000 or more. The contracting officer can approve all modifications that exercise contract options and modifications that do not increase costs or product

delivery completion dates. The individual responsible for certifying RFCs, or if he/she desires one lower management level, must certify cumulative changes that increase the contract cost up to $24,999; or extend contract completion or delivery dates.

major modifications are cumulative changes that increase the current contract cost by $25,000 or more. The individual responsible for certifying RFCs must certify major modifications.

Documentation for requesting certification of major modifications includes:

a description of the new work and new deliverables, that caused a major modification,

an explanation as to why the new work was not included in the original RFC or a detailed explanation of other reasons the modification is necessary,

a summary of all prior modifications to the contract, and

reasons why additional modifications will not be necessary or reasons why additional modifications will be necessary.

Modifications that are outside the intent of the original scope of work should be processed as a new procurement.

*8-15-60 Acquisition and Management of Consultant Services Obtained Through Purchase Order*

Purchase orders are used for acquiring consultant services that cost less than $10,000. Consultant services that cost less than $10,000 are subject to the provisions of this Chapter as modified by the following paragraphs.

A. The provisions of Paragraph 8-15-40A, "Budgeting for consultant services," are not applicable.

B. The provisions of Paragraph 8-15-40B, "Requests for consultant services," and Exhibit X8-15-4 are applicable. In addition, POC and OS staff office heads and, in regions, PROs will take the actions necessary to ensure that consultant services projects are not segmented to avoid the controls and provisions contained in this Chapter.

C. The provisions of Paragraph 8-15-40C, "Certifying requests for contracts," are applicable except that the individual responsible for certifying RFCs may delegate this responsibility to any departmental official except the project officer or the individual authorized to enter into the purchase order agreement. However, the individual responsible for certifying RFCs must certify purchase orders if consultant services are purchased from the same individual or firm more than three times in any twelve month period by the same program or administrative office.

D. The provisions of Paragraph 8-15-40D, "Procurement of consultant services," are applicable except that HEW procurement regulations 3-3.6 govern the use of purchase orders and purchase orders will not be reported to DCIS. To monitor the use of purchase orders, the DASGP requests that POCs, OS staff offices and regions report each December 15 the number of consultant purchase orders and the cost of purchase orders used during the preceding fiscal year.

E. The provisions of Paragraph 8-15-40E, "Administration of consultant service contracts," are applicable at the discretion of the individual responsible for certifying RFCs.

F. The provisions of Paragraph 8-15-40F, "Assessing and using consultant services deliverable products," are applicable except that an assessment report (Exhibit X8-15-5) is not required.

G. The provisions of Section 8-15-50, "Contract modifications," are applicable except the individual responsible for certifying the purchase order must certify changes that impact costs and changes that increase completion dates or product delivery dates.

*8-15-70 Implementation*

The Assistant Secretary for Management and Budget and the Assistant Secretary for Planning and Evaluation will monitor the implementation of this Chapter and the processes and reporting prescribed.

POC and OS staff office heads and PROs will issue such additional instructions as are necessary to implement the requirements described in this chapter and will provide the instructions to the ASMB for the review and comment.

## Exclusions

The following are not considered consultant services:

**1.** Basic research, applied research and development (as defined by the National Science Foundation) including clinical, biomedical, and behavioral projects, and contracts needed to directly support these projects. In addition, surveys conducted in direct support of basic research, applied research, and development projects. However, this does not mean that every project of an agency conducting clinical, biomedical or behavioral research is excluded; for example, evaluations of research projects and other consultant services are not excluded; and projects that combine limited research and consultant services are not excluded.

**2.** Specific program functions established by statute to be performed by a consultant. In addition the following operations and program functions are excluded:

Operation of national clearinghouses.

Operation of national program reporting systems that are required by statute to be performed by a consultant.

Operation of professional standards review organizations.

Operation of drug abuse centers.

Operation of day care centers.

Head Start career development and assistance to Head Start grantees.

Intermediaries employed in support of Medicare and Medicaid.

**3.** Services that are excluded include:

Testing services performed by FDA and CDC in support of regulatory functions.

Services performed in support of the Indian Self Determination Act PL 93-638.

Services performed by national commissions, advisory committees or groups, review panels, boards, and committees.

Services performed by physicians, attorneys, and similar professional, para-professionals, or experts in the individual disability of other claimant determination; or such services rendered in support of grievances, arbitrations, appeals, hearings, adjudication of direct dealing Medicare claims and for medical reconsideration of Medicare beneficiary claims.

Services provided by field readers.

Services provided by subcontractors or consultants under a prime contract.

Services provided by State and local government or their designated agents.

Services and technical assistance to grantees or to State and local governments or their designated agents.

Services provided by other Federal agencies, or other HEW activities.

Services obtained through grants.

**4.** Administrative support services that are excluded include:

Direct health services and employee health services.

Housekeeping and maintenance services.

Architect and engineering services related to construction.

Transcription services, captioned film and news clipping services.

Microfilm and copying services and mailing and distribution services.

Routine literature searching, indexing and abstracting services.

Data reduction and verification services (keypunch, key to tape, or disk, etc.).

Data processing services (rental of computer equipment time, and the management and operation of a facility, and rental of "off the shelf" software packages).

Programming services that do not require analysis.

Communications services.

## Congressional Budget Estimate of Consultant Services Guidelines

(Explanations are keyed to the reference numbers set forth in the attached report format)

This form will be used to submit Congressional budget estimates.

(1) Indicate the appropriate fiscal year.
(2) Fill in the individual POC name, all OS staff offices or all regions.
(3) Identify education component (ASE, NIP, OE) and PHS component (FDA, HSA, HRA, ADAMHA, CDC, NIH or ASH).
(4) Fill in SSA, OE, HCFA bureau or comparable level and OS staff office (ASPE, OCR, OCA, IG and DM for all others).
(5) The A, B, C and D categories are described in Section 8-15-20. Appointive consultants is self explanatory.
(6) Estimate amount of consultant services dollars for each consultant service category consistent with ASMB zero base budget instructions. Provide minimum, current and incremental funding levels.
(7) Total estimated dollars. Provide totals at level of organization or budget activity described in (4) above, agency totals, and POC totals.
(8) Justify why the work is required and why the work cannot be done in-house. Avoid stereotype justifications.

If at any time, any POC, OS staff office or region expects that it will exceed the estimate by more than 5 percent, a memorandum should be sent to the Deputy Assistant Secretary, Finance. This should contain the current estimate, the proposed increase, and an explanation which outlines the assumptions used for the original or current estimate and the new assumptions and reasons for the increase.

Fiscal Year ( 1.) _____ Budget Estimate
(Name of Principal Operating Component) ( 2.)
(Name of Agency) ( 3.)
(In Thousands of Dollars)
(Bureau or comparable organization) ( 4.)

| Consultant Services Categories (5.) | Estimated Amount (6.) | | | Explanation of Need to Use Consultants (8.) |
|---|---|---|---|---|
| | Minimum | Current | Incremental | |
| a. Services for internal operation | _____ | _____ | _____ | _____ |
| b. Direct support services | _____ | _____ | _____ | _____ |
| c. Survey services | _____ | _____ | _____ | _____ |
| d. Evaluation services | _____ | _____ | _____ | _____ |
| e. Appointive consultants | _____ | _____ | _____ | _____ |
| TOTAL ESTIMATES (7.) | _____ | _____ | _____ | _____ |

## Consultant Service Plan

Each POC or OS staff office head and Principal Regional Official (PRO) will prepare a consultant services plan. The plan will describe and justify individual projects that will require the use of consultant services during the next fiscal year. The Assistant Secretary for Management and Budget (ASMB) will issue instructions for preparation of the consultant services plan. The Assistant Secretary for Planning and Evaluation (ASPE) will issue additional instructions for the evaluation and survey portions of the plan. The plan will be provided to the Assistant Secretary for Management and Budget (ASMB) in September, just prior to the start of the fiscal year. The evaluation and survey portions of the plan will be provided through the ASPE and they should be drawn from the Agency Research, Evaluation and Statistical plans. The ASMB will review the consultant services plan to ensure POCs, OS staff offices and regions are within expenditure ceilings. After forwarding the consultant services plan, a copy of the plan should be used by the program or administrative offices and the procurement office to develop the fiscal year procurement plan required by the Secretary. Preparation of the consultant services plan should not preclude or interfere with first quarter consultant procurements. Accordingly, program and administrative offices can prepare and certify first quarter RFCs provided the project is included in the POC, OS staff office or regions consultant services plan.

If at any time, any POC, OS staff office or region expects that it will exceed its plan estimate by more than 5 percent, a memorandum should be sent to the Deputy Assistant Secretary, Finance. This should contain the current estimate, the proposed increase, and an explanation which outlines the assumptions used for the original or current estimate and the new assumptions and reasons for the increase.

The plan consists of individual projects and the summary costs of projects.

The individual project justification is described at page 2 and 3 of this exhibit. A plan is required for each project over $10,000.

The format and instructions for summarized costs of projects are at pages 4 and 5.

## Project Description and Justification

**1.** Agency Proposing: (Agency and Bureau)

**2.** Date: (Indicate if revision)

**3.** Consultant Service Budget ID: (Provide a unique, centrally-assigned identifying number showing POC, agency or OS staff office fiscal year of initiation and a three digit number, e.g., (ADAMHA-77-001, ADAMHA-77-002, etc.). For POC, agency, or OS staff office identification, use the following identifiers: FDA, HSA, Institute of NIH (e.g., NCI), ADAMHA, HRA, ASH, OE, ASE, NIE, HCFA, SRS, SSA, OHD, and for OS staff offices, use ASPE, OCR, REG (Regional), OCA, IG, and DM for all others.

**4.** Category: (Indicate whether contract is for services for A—internal operations, B—direct support services, C—survey services, or D—evaluation services. Paragraph 8-15-20 defines categories A, B, C, and D.)

**5.** Project Title: (Title and a one to two sentence description of the project.)

**6.** Cost and Funding Source: (Estimated cost for prior, current, and next fiscal year and each appropriation to be used.)

**7.** Execution: Provide rationale for not doing project in-house. Indicate the agency and bureau under which the project will be administered, the planned time-frame, or phases or milestones, and end products.

**8.** Contact: (Name, address, and telephone number of the person responsible for developing project.)

**9.** Coordination: (Identify the agencies, offices or persons that have or will review the project. Indicate whether such review has occurred or will occur. If the former, indicate views and problems identified.)

**10.** Background and Purpose: (Provide information on genesis and basis of the problem to which project is addressed, on prior history of the project and on general purpose of the project.)

**11.** Related Work: (Discuss related work completed, under way, or proposed, which bears on the approach or expected impact of the project. Specifically indicate (a) how the project will build on the strengths or weaknesses of such work and (b) how the project will provide additional information not now available to the Department. Show that no products already exist which could meet the objectives of the project by checking, as appropriate, sources such as Evaluation Documentation Center, the Policy Analysis Source Book, NTIS, DCIS, specialized information systems, and experts in other agencies.)

**12.** Approach: (Describe the approach to be employed in the project. Include a discussion, whenever relevant, of the population to be examined; type of data to be examined or collected; data gathering methods; analytic tools or techniques; and relationship of the study population to the total universe. Show that the approach proposed is likely to be adequate to obtain the expected results and why it is selected over alternatives. Show also that lower-cost alternatives are not available. "Alternative" means alternatives to scope or approach, not in-house versus contract.)

**13.** Expected Findings: (Briefly describe, as applicable, (a) the questions to be answered and/or the hypotheses to be tested, and (b) the expected findings.)

**14.** Application and Utilization of Findings: (Briefly describe (a) the relationships of the expected results of end products to specific HEW programs and the decision makers who will use the results, (b) the expected actions to be taken by whom, and (c) the effects of these actions on the population served.

Show that these results, actions and effects are (d) important and significant enough to the Department to justify the project costs, and (e) present plans for dissemination and utilization of the final product.)

**15.** RFC Date: (Complete after this project is approved. Date contract is planned to be awarded.)

## Consultant Service Plan Summary Costs Guidelines

(Explanations are keyed to the reference numbers set forth in the attached report format)

(**1**) Indicate the appropriate fiscal year.
(**2**) Fill in individual POC, all OS staff offices or all regions,
(**3**) Fill in education component (ASE, NIE or OE) or PHS component (FDA, HRA, HSA, ADAMHA, CDC, NIH or ASH),
(**4**) Fill in SSA, OE, HCFA bureau or component level and OS staff offices (ASPE, OCR, OCA, IG and DM for all others),
(**5**) The categories are as described in paragraph 8-15-20.
(**6**) Estimate amount of consultant services plan dollars for each consultant service category.
(**7**) Total estimated dollars. Provide totals at level of organization or budget activity described in (**4**) above, agency totals, and POC totals.

CONSULTANT SERVICES PLAN SUMMARY COST
Fiscal Year (1.) _____
(Name of Principal Operating Component) (2.)
(Name of Agency) (3.)
(In Thousands of Dollars)
(Bureau or comparable organization) (4.)

| Consultant Services Categories (5.) | Estimated Amount (6.) |
| --- | --- |
| a. Services for internal operation | _____ |
| b. Direct support services | _____ |
| c. Survey services | _____ |
| d. Evaluation services | _____ |
| e. Appointive consultants | _____ |
|    TOTAL ESTIMATES (7.) | _____ |

## Requests for Consultant Services

When developing the RFC there are seven key points which the sponsoring office must consider:

First, where the work to be performed requires substantial further definition by the contractor and where there are alternative methods for accomplishing the work the RFC will state that the successful contractor will, as an early deliverable, provide two approaches with associated cost of each for accomplishing the work. The purpose of this requirement is to provide the sponsoring office an opportunity to evaluate approaches and to select objectives at the least cost.

Second, if the state of the art is unproven or if the work approach is untested, then the RFC should state the contractor will deliver a feasibility study, simulation test or other evidence that demonstrates that the project can be successfully completed using the recommended approach.

Third, when the development of survey forms is part of a consultant service, the work statement should be written to ensure that the contractor is constructively employed during the government clearance process. If forms clearance may require an extended period of time, the contractor should receive only the minimum reimbursement necessary to retain key personnel.

Fourth, the RFC should minimally provide for a monthly status report that describes work accomplished; work scheduled on tasks for the next reporting period; current and anticipated problems that will impact on the performance of the contractor; and for cost type contracts, the cost to date of performing the tasks as well as a cumulative cost to complete the project.

Fifth, the RFC should include the project purpose, objectives and either detail work requirements or a provision for the contractor to deliver a detail work plan that will achieve the purpose and objectives. In either event the program or administrative project officer must state what he intends to accomplish in the RFC.

Sixth, the schedule for completing work events and providing deliverable products should be specified in the request for contract (RFC). The description of deliverable products or a separate section should provide for acceptance criteria for deliverables.

Seventh, the request for contract should be carefully developed to ensure that it is conducive to competition; is competitive; and will not need major modifications.

## Report on Assessment of Benefits
## Received from Consultant Services

GUIDELINES FOR PREPARING REPORT

(Explanations are keyed to the reference numbers set forth in the attached "Report on Assessment of Consultant Services Rendered")

The data to be furnished is in response to congressional requirements. Use as much detail as necessary to respond to the report requirements.

Do not combine awards. Each award identified should be treated as a separate report. This requirement does not apply to contracts that are less than $25,000 or purchase orders.

( 1 ) Indicate your POC, Agency, and Bureau.

( 2 ) Self explanatory

( 3 ) Self explanatory

( 4 ) Indicate the consultant service budget ID number as it appeared in the consultant service plan. *

( 5 ) Provide project title from the consultant services plan. Supplement with final report title if different.

( 6 ) Check appropriate box. Explain how the purposes or objectives were or were not achieved. In this regard you should explain how well the products satisfied acceptance criteria.

( 7 ) Explain the impact of the consultant findings or recommendations. In this regard the program office needs to describe the use of the products that was anticipated when the request for contract was certified; state if the intended use of the product has been modified as a result of the contract; and provide a timetable during which major implementation actions will occur.

Assessments must be accomplished no later than 120 days after physical completion of the award.

Submit Reports to:

Director, Division of Financial Planning
    and Analysis
HEW South Portal, Room 745D
330 Independence Ave., S.W.
Washington, D.C. 20201

* A budget identification number will not be available for contract modifications made in FY 1976 and subsequent years against awards initially issued prior to FY 1976 and for any awards or modifications not previously presented in the budget.

## Report on Assessment of Consultant Services Rendered

( 1 ) POC, Agency, and Bureau

( 2 ) Name and Address of Awardee

( 3 ) Award Number

( 4 ) Budget Identification

( 5 ) Project Title

( 6 ) Was the purpose or major object for this award achieved?
Yes ____ No ____
Explain.

( 7 ) What impact have the consultant's findings or recommendations had or will have on the emphasis, direction and content of the program or project?

## LETTER AGREEMENT

(Letterhead)

_____, 198_

(Name and address of consultant)

Dear _____:

    1. _Term._ I am pleased to confirm your appointment as a consultant to _____ (The Corporation) to serve in connection with the _____ project.

**For retention of consultant for a specific period:**

1.  _Term._ I am pleased to confirm your appointment as a consultant to _____ (The Corporation) for the period _____ to _____.

**For retention of consultant on a continuing basis:**

1.  _Appointment._ I am pleased to confirm your appointment as a consultant to _____ (The Corporation).

2.  _Services._ You shall perform such work or services as are set forth in Exhibit A, attached hereto and specifically made a part of this Agreement. The work or services to be performed by you may be changed by the Corporation from time to time by letter requests sent to you. You shall keep the Corporation informed of the progress of any work being performed under this Agreement.

3.  _Compensation and Expenses._
    (a) The Corporation will pay you a total fee of $_____ for all work performed hereunder on satisfactory completion of the work.

**For retention of consultant for a specific period:**

3.  (a) Your compensation will be at the rate of $_____ per month for all work performed hereunder. You will be paid at the same time you are reimbursed for approved expenses under paragraph 3(b) below.

**For retention of consultant on a continuing basis:**

3. (a) Your compensation will be at the rate of $_____ per (hour) (day) and will be based on the submission of Certification of Work Forms (enclosed) on a monthly basis. You will be paid at the same time that you are reimbursed for approved expenses under paragraph 3(b) below.

   (b) You will receive reimbursement for the actual cost of reasonable expenses arising out of the work performed under this Agreement [not to exceed $_____], subject to the approval of the Corporation. You shall deliver an intemized statement to the Corporation on a monthly basis that shows fully the work being performed under this Agreement and all related expenses. The Corporation will pay you the amount of any authorized expenses within thirty (30) days of the receipt of the itemized statement of all expenses, submitted together with receipts for all hotel, car rental, air fare, and other transportation expenses and for all other expenses of $25.00 or more.

4. *Working Facilities.* You will be furnished with such facilities and services as shall be suitable for your position and adequate for the performance of your duties under this Agreement.

5. *Reports.* Any and all reports, manuscripts, and any other work product, whether completed or not, that are prepared or developed by you as a part of the work under this Agreement shall be the property of the Corporation and shall be turned over to the Corporation promptly at the Corporation's request or at the termination of this Agreement, whichever is earlier.

6. *Independent Contractor.* You shall exercise control over the means and manner in which you perform any work requested hereunder, and in all respects your relationship to the Corporation shall be that of an independent contractor serving as a consultant and not as an employee.

7. *Termination.* This Agreement may be terminated upon thirty (30) days' written notice by either party.

8. *Confidential Information.* You agree that for the term of your appointment hereunder and for two (2) years thereafter, that you

will not disclose to any person, firm, or corporation any confidential information regarding the Corporation, its businesses, directors, officers, and employees.

**For retention of consultant on a continuing basis:**
8. *Confidential Information.* You agree that while you are serving as a consultant to the Corporation and for two (2) years after you have given or received notice of termination under paragraph 7 above you will not disclose to any person, firm, or corporation any confidential information regarding the Corporation, its businesses, directors, officers, and employees.

9. *Nonassignable.* This Agreement is personal in nature and is not assignable by you or by the Corporation.

**Transferable from the corporation to a related enterprise:**
9. *Assignments.* Performance by you under this Agreement is personal in nature, and this Agreement is not assignable by you. The Corporation may assign this Agreement to any subsidiary, affiliate, or related enterprise upon written notice to you.

**Assignable by the consultant:**
9. *Assignments.* With the prior written consent of the Corporation, you may assign this Agreement and the benefits and obligation hereunder to any person, including a corporation, of equal responsibility to you. The consent of the Corporation may not be withheld unreasonably.

10. *Arbitration.* Any controversy or claim arising out of or relating to this Agreement or the breach thereof shall be settled at _____ in accordance with the rules then obtaining of the American Arbitration Association, and judgment upon the award may be entered in any court having jurisdiction thereof. This Agreement constitutes the voluntary submission of both parties to such arbitration.

11. *Entire Agreement.* This letter, including Exhibit A, contains the entire agreement of the parties. It may not be changed orally but

only by an agreement signed by the party against whom enforcement of any waiver, change, modification, extension, or discharge is sought.

12. *Approval.* I trust that the terms of this appointment meet with your approval. If so, please indicate this by signing a copy of this letter and returning it to the Corporation. An additional copy of this letter is enclosed for your records.

Very truly yours,

By _____

Accepted and Agreed to this
_____ day of _____ , 198__.

_____
(signed)

## EXHIBIT A

This is attached to and made a part of the Letter Agreement, dated \_\_\_\_
\_\_\_\_, 198\_\_ between _____ (the Corporation) and _____
(the Consultant).

The Consultant will evaluate the record-keeping systems currently
utilized by the Corporation in the Corporation's material's handling
division pertaining to inventory control and will recommend
improvements in these systems.

    The evaluation will include, but not be limited to:

1.  A review of the records being generated on a regular basis.
2.  Evaluation of storage and access systems.
3.  Examination of long-term retention systems and standards.

    The written recommendations must include specific
recommendations on at least the following:

A.  Which records being generated can be eliminated.
B.  In what form should the current records be kept, i.e. hard copy,
    microfilm, and/or computer memory.
C.  How long should records be kept available in the work place.
D.  When current records should be sent to long term storage and in
    what form.
E.  When current records can be destroyed.
F.  Which records, if any, must be kept indefinitely.

The written recommendations include evaluations of the costs and
benefits of implementing each or all of the changes recommended.

    The written recommendations are to be delivered to the Corporation
within 120 days of the date of the Letter Agreement.

## MASTER CONSULTING CONTRACT

This contract sets forth the terms and conditions under which The Service Company ("TSC") proposes to use the services of _____ _____, Inc. ("Consultant") from time to time to perform work or services ("Work") as described in work requests from TSC's representative hereunder, all such Work to be performed on the following basis and subject to the following terms and conditions:

1. TSC shall have the right from time to time to request in writing that Consultant or certain employees of Consultant perform consulting work (the "Work") for TSC, provided, however, Consultant shall have the right to refuse any work request by notifying TSC within ten (10) days after receipt of the work request.

### Optional paragraph 1:

1. All of the work or service to be performed by Consultant for TSC under this Agreement (hereinafter collectively referred to as the "Work") are more fully described in Schedule A, attached hereto and by this reference specifically made a part hereof:

2. Unless TSC shall specify otherwise in writing, all requests for Work to be performed hereunder shall be made in writing by _____, who shall, in all respects, be considered TSC's Representative hereunder. In the event of _____'s absence or incapacity, _____ is designated TSC's Alternate Representative. Consultant shall keep TSC or its Representatives informed of the progress of the work being performed hereunder.

3. Attached hereto as Schedule A, and by this reference specifically made a part hereof, is a schedule of fees and other costs to be paid by TSC in connection with any work that may be performed by Consultant for TSC. Schedule A may be updated from time to time by Consultant whenever it becomes necessary to change the fees set forth therein. Whenever such a revised Schedule A has been received by TSC, the revised Schedule A shall replace the prior Schedule A and by this reference shall become a part of this Agreement between TSC and Consultant, provided, however, no revision of Schedule A shall be in effect regarding any work requests then outstanding.

**Optional paragraph 3:**

3. TSC shall pay Consultant for the Work performed hereunder the sum of (a) a fixed monthly fee of _____ thousand dollars ($          ) plus (b) recoverable costs as set forth in Schedule B attached hereto and by this reference made a part hereof.

4 (a) TSC shall pay Consultant a fee for all work performed hereunder, such fee to be calculated on the basis of the fees set forth in Schedule A, attached hereto. Itemized statements shall be delivered to TSC on a monthly basis and shall show fully the task being performed, the individual(s) performing the task, the title of such individual(s), and the man-days involved. Such statement shall also include, in itemized form, Consultant's authorized expenses arising out of its performance of the work requested by TSC. TSC agrees to pay Consultant the amount of such statements within thirty (30) days after receipt thereof, provided, however, Consultant shall notify immediately TSC in writing when the fees and authorized expenses arising out of its performance of the Work under any work request exceed $____.

4 (b) In addition to the basic fee and costs herein agreed to be paid to the Consultant for Work hereunder, TSC shall pay the Consultant the direct fees and authorized costs, as defined in Schedule A, incurred by the Consultant in performing any additional work or services requested in writing by TSC's Representative and not required to be performed by the Consultant under this Agreement.

**Optional paragraph 4:**

4. Statements shall be delivered to TSC on a monthly basis and shall show the nature of the Work performed, the individual(s) performing the task, the title of such individual(s) and the man-days involved. Such statements shall also include, in itemized form, Consultant's recoverable costs arising out of its performance of the Work. TSC agrees to pay Consultant the amount of such statements within fifteen (15) days after receipt thereof.

5. Any and all reports, manuscripts, or any other work product, whether completed or not, which are prepared or developed by Consultant as part of the work requested by TSC hereunder, shall be the property of TSC and shall be turned over to TSC promptly at TSC's request or at the termination of this agreement, whichever is earlier.

6. Except as provided below, TSC shall have the right to and shall own any and all patentable or copyrightable inventions, processes, plans, or techniques, together with any applications for patents or copyrights and the patents and the copyrights that may issue thereunder, which are created, developed, or invented by Consultant or any of its employees as a result of or arising out of the Work requested by TSC hereunder. At TSC's request and expense, Consultant agrees to do or cause to be done all things necessary to enable TSC to require the full right to the use and ownership of any and all the rights and properties described hereinabove in this paragraph 6.

7. In the performance of the Work, Consultant may acquire or be made aware of certain confidential information, in particular, but not limited to, confidential information relating to the Work regarding products, processes, and operations as well as present and contemplated activities of TSC. Consultant, its employees, and others whose services may be procured by Consultant to assist Consultant in the performance of the Work shall not divulge or disclose such confidential information to others without first having obtained specific written permission from TSC to do so. The term "confidential information" as used herein shall mean information disclosed to Consultant by TSC or information obtained by Consultant for TSC in the course of performing the Work hereunder, excluding information previously known to Consultant or information that is publicly known (except through disclosure of Consultant in violation of this paragraph) or information that comes to Consultant by right from a third party without confidential commitment.

8. Consultant shall save, indemnify, and hold TSC harmless from all liability, claims, suits, judgments, damages, and losses growing out of any infringement of any patent or patent rights or copyrights covering any equipment, machine, applicance, operation, or method of operation practiced by Consultant, in the performance of the Work requested hereunder by TSC.

9. All employees of Consultant engaged in any of the Work performed by TSC hereunder at all times and in all places shall be subject to the sole direction, supervision, and control of Consultant. Consultant shall exercise control over the means and manner in which it and its employees perform the Work requested by TSC hereunder, and in all respects Consultant's relationship and the relationship of all of Con-

sultant's employees to TSC shall be that of an independent contractor.

10. Consultant shall indemnify and forever hold and save TSC harmless against any and all suits, causes of action, claims, liabilities, damages, or losses resulting from the acts or conduct of Consultant or its agents and employees, regardless of the character of the acts or conduct and asserted by anyone whomsoever, resulting from the performance of the Work requested hereunder, and for which the Consultant or its agents and employees are legally responsible.

**Optional paragraph 10:**

10. Consultant shall be liable only for any failure to perform in accordance with generally accepted professional standards and the standards imposed by law. Consultant shall have no liability under this agreement unless the claim is made in writing within one (1) year after Consultant's completion of Work. Consultant's liability to TSC for any loss or damage arising out of or in connection with this Agreement from any cause, including Consultant's negligence, shall not exceed the total fixed monthly fees received by Consultant hereunder, and TSC hereby releases Consultant from any liability in excess of such amount. Under no circumstances shall Consultant be liable to TSC for any consequential or incidental damages including, but not limited to, loss of use or loss of profit, whether or not caused by Consultant's fault or negligence.

11. Unless TSC shall specify otherwise in writing, notices, statements, and all other matters concerning the Work to be performed hereunder shall be addressed to TSC as follows:

Unless Consultant shall specify otherwise in writing, notices, requests for service, and all other matters concerning the Work to be performed hereunder shall be addressed to Consultant as follows:

Any and all notices or other communications required or permitted by this Agreement or by law to be served on or given to either party hereto by the other party hereto shall be in writing and shall be deemed duly served and given upon actual receipt by the party to whom it is directed.

12. There is incorporated herein by reference, Section 202 of Executive Order 11,246, dated September 24, 1965, as amended, to the general effect that Consultant shall not discriminate against any employee or applicant for employment under this agreement because of race, color, religion, sex, or national origin, and further that Consultant shall take affirmative action to insure that applicants and employees are treated without regard to their race, color, religion, sex, or national origin.

13. Notwithstanding any other provision hereof, TSC or Consultant may cancel this agreement upon written notice to the other party, provided, however, Consultant may not terminate any Work requested by TSC and not rejected by the Consultant as provided for in paragraph 1 herein by Consultant prior to Consultant's notice of termination hereunder, unless TSC shall so consent. TSC may, however, direct Consultant to terminate any Work at any time, or TSC may suspend Consultant's performance temporarily hereunder or on a specific project hereunder at any time or from time to time. TSC's only obligation under this paragraph 13 for any such cancellation, cessation, suspension, or redirection of the Work being performed by Consultant shall be the payment to Consultant of the fees and authorized expenses for the Work actually performed.

**Optional paragraph 13:**

13. Notwithstanding any other provision hereof, either party may cancel this Agreement upon written notice to the other party. Upon written notice, however, TSC may direct Consultant to terminate any of the Work at any time, or TSC may suspend temporarily Consultant's performance hereunder at any time or from time to time. TSC's only obligation under this paragraph 13 for any such cancellation, cessation, suspension, or redirection of the Work being performed by Consultant shall be the payment to Consultant of the fee for the Work actually performed.

14. This agreement is personal in nature and is not assignable by either TSC or Consultant. Consultant may subcontract portions of its

requested Work or services upon approval of the proposed subcontractor by TSC, provided such approval shall not relieve Consultant of its responsibility under this agreement for the Work.

## First optional paragraph 14:

14 (a) This Agreement is personal in nature and is not assignable by either Consultant or TSC. Consultant may, however, subcontract its services, in whole or in part, to others without the prior approval of TSC. Consultant hereby guarantees to TSC compliance by such other persons with the responsibilities and liabilities herein assumed by Consultant, provided that the limitations on Consultant's liability set forth in the Agreement constitute the aggregate limit of liability of Consultant and its subcontractors to TSC and TSC agrees to hold only Consultant responsible for any failure to so comply. Consultant agrees that TSC will incur no duplication of costs as a result of any such subcontract.

(b) Neither Party hereto shall be considered in default in the performance of its obligations hereunder to the extent that the performance of any such obligation is prevented or delayed by any cause, existing or future, beyond the reasonable control of the affected party, provided however, that the settlement of strikes and lockouts shall be entirely within the discretion of the Party having the difficulty.

## Second optional paragraph 14:

14. Either party may assign its rights or delegate its duties under this Agreement with the prior written approval of the other party, provided, however, that such approval shall not relieve Consultant of its responsibility under the Agreement for the Work. Consultant may subcontract portions of the Work without the prior approval of TSC, provided, however, that such subcontracting shall not relieve Consultant of its responsibility under this Agreement for the Work.

15. Consultant, its employees, and others whose services may be procured by Consultant to assist Consultant in the performance of the Work shall agree to be bound by the terms of paragraphs 5, 6, 7, 8, and 14 herein, unless waived in writing by TSC.

16. During the term of this Agreement, Consultant shall reveal promptly to TSC all matters coming to its attention pertaining to the business of TSC and shall not accept similar employment from, or serve in a similar capacity with, any other concern that is at such time engaged in a business of a like or similar nature to the business now conducted by TSC.

17. During the term of this Agreement, and for _____ years thereafter, Consultant shall not reveal to outside sources, without the written consent of TSC, any matters, the reveal of which may, in any manner, adversely affect TSC's business, unless required by law to do so.

18. Consultant will take out and maintain all insurance required by any governmental unit to meet any statutory requirement and to protect Consultant and TSC fully from and against any and all claims arising out of the Work performed hereunder. Consultant will supply TSC with satisfactory evidence thereof. The cost of such insurance shall not be deemed an authorized expense for the Work.

**Optional paragraph 18:**

18. Consultant will take out and maintain all insurance required by any governmental unit to meet any statutory requirement, to protect Consultant and TSC fully from and against any and all claims arising out of the Work performed hereunder, and as requested by TSC. Consultant will supply TSC with satisfactory evidence thereof. The cost of such insurance shall be deemed a Recoverable Cost of the Work as set forth in Exhibit B attached hereto.

19. This Agreement shall be governed by and construed in accordance with the laws of the State of _____.

20. The United States District Court for the _____ District of _____ shall have jurisdiction with respect to all matters hereunder, and Consultant and TSC hereby submit themselves to the jurisdiction of the United States District Court for the _____ District of _____ for all purposes; provided, however, if the said court shall lack jurisdiction, the (_____ State) Court shall have jurisdiction with respect to all matters hereunder and the parties hereby submit

themselves to the jurisdiction of the (_____ State) Court for all purposes.

21. Any waiver, alteration, or modification of any of the provisions of this Agreement shall not be valid unless in writing and signed by the parties.

## Optional paragraph 21(b):

21 (b) No waiver by either party of any defaults of the other party under this Agreement shall operate as a waiver of any future default, whether of a like or different character.

22. This instrument contains the entire Agreement between TSC and the Consultant, and any agreement or representation respecting the duties of either TSC or the Consultant hereunder not expressly set forth in this instrument is null and void.

## Optional paragraph 22(b):

22 (b) If any term or provision of this Agreement or the application thereof to any person or circumstance shall, to any extent, be invalid or unenforceable, the remainder of this Agreement, or the application of such term or provision to persons or circumstances other than those as to which it is held invalid or unenforceable, shall not be affected thereby and each term and provision of this Agreement shall be valid and be enforced to the fullest extent permitted by law.

TSC

By _____

Consultant

By _____

## SCHEDULE A

To Agreement between TSC and _____Dated _____, 198__
The Work performed under this Agreement will be on a billing-rate basis in accordance with the following rate structure:

*Number of Days    Rate per Day*
$

Partial days will be prorated on an hourly basis.

The above rates cover all direct labor. Expenses incurred, such as travel, subsistance, copying, etc., will be billed at cost.

## SCHEDULE B

### Recoverable Costs

TSC shall reimburse Consultant for all reasonable costs and expenses incurred by Consultant in the performance of the Work. Such costs and expenses generally include but are not limited to the following:

1. *Payroll and Related Personnel Costs.* Costs and related expenses incurred by Consultant in accordance with its established personnel policies, including all salaries and wages of personnel engaged directly in the performance of the Work, plus TSC's established rate for payroll additives to cover all employee benefits and allowances for vacation, sick leave, holiday, and company portion of employee insurance and retirement benefits, all payroll taxes, premiums for public liability and property damage liability insurance, Worker's Compensation and employer's liability insurance and all other insurance premiums measured by payroll costs, and other contributions and benefits imposed by any applicable law or regulation. Said rate for payroll additives shall be subject to adjustment annually to reflect increased costs as verified by Consultant's independent auditors.

2. *Overhead Expenses.* Rent, leasehold improvements and expenses, office equipment, fixtures, and supplies.

3. *Other Direct Costs.* All other costs incurred in the performance of the Work, including such costs as:
   (a) Travel, subsistence, relocation, and return of personnel engaged in the performance of the Work.
   (b) The costs of all materials and supplies used in the performance of the Work.
   (c) Costs for reproduction of plans, specifications, reports, and other data and for models at Consultant's standard rate.
   (d) Computer services, including related operator time, keypunching, and machine time and related computer services for all other hardware or programs at cost to Consultant.
   (e) Communications expenses, at cost to Consultant.
   (f) Subcontracts and other outside services and facilities, at cost to Consultant.

(g) All taxes and assessments incurred in connection with the performance of the services under this Agreement and paid by Consultant, excepting only taxes levied directly on or measured by net income and corporate franchise taxes.

(h) Insurance and bonding costs, fees and expenses.

## DEPARTMENT OF HOUSING AND URBAN DEVELOPMENT
## PROFESSIONAL SERVICES CONTRACTS

The following are typical contract terms required in all contracts for engineering, architectural, planning, and other professional services funded with Community Development Funds from the U.S. Department of Housing and Urban Development. All contracts include paragraphs 6 through 12: the first five sections are optional but may be required by the local government in awarding the contract.

**1.** *Termination of Contract for Cause.* If, through any cause, the Consultant shall fail to fulfill in timely and proper manner his obligations under this Contract, or if the Consultant shall violate any of the covenants, agreements, or stipulations of this Contract, the Public Body thereupon shall have the right to terminate this contract by giving written notice to the Consultant of such termination and specifying the effective date thereof, at least five days before the effective date of such termination. In such event, all finished or unfinished documents, data, studies, and reports prepared by the Consultant under this Contract shall, at the option of the Public Body, become its property and the Consultant shall be entitled to receive just and equitable compensation for any satisfactory work completed on such documents.

Notwithstanding the above, the Consultant shall not be relieved of liability to the Public Body for damages sustained by the Public Body by virtue of any breach of the Contract by the Consultant, and the Public Body may withhold any payments to the Consultant for the purpose of setoff until such time as the exact amount of damages due the Public Body from the Consultant is determined.

**2.** *Termination for Convenience of Public Body.* The Public Body may terminate this contract any time by a notice in writing from the Public Body to the Consultant. If the Contract is terminated by the Public Body as provided herein, the Consultant will be paid an amount that bears the same ratio to the total compensation as the services actually performed bear to the total services of the Consultant covered by this Contract, less payments of compensation previously made: *Provided,* however, that if less than 60 percent of the services covered by this Contract have been performed upon the effective date of such termination, the Consultant shall be reimbursed (in addition to the above payment) for that portion of the actual out-of-pocket expenses (not otherwise reimbursed under this Contract) incurred by the Consultant during the Contract period directly attributable to the uncompleted portion of the services covered by this Contract.

If this Contract is terminated due to the fault of the Consultant, Section 1 hereof relative to termination shall apply.

3. *Changes.* The Public Body may, from time to time, request changes in the scope of the services of the Consultant to be performed hereunder. Such changes, including any increase or decrease in the amount of the Consultant's compensation, which are mutually agreed upon by and between the Public Body and the Consultant, shall be incorporated in written amendments to this Contract.

4. *Compliance with Local Laws.* The Consultant shall comply with all applicable laws, ordinances, and codes of the state and local governments, and shall commit no trespass on any public or private property in performing any of the work embraced by this Contract.

5. *Assignability.* The Consultant shall not assign any interest in this Contract, and shall not transfer any interest in the same (whether by assignment or novation) without the prior written approval of the Public Body: *Provided,* however, that claims for money due or to become due the Consultant from the Public Body under this Contract may be assigned to a bank, trust company, or other financial institution, or to a Trustee in Bankruptcy, without such approval. Notice of any such assignment or transfer shall be furnished promptly to the Public Body.

6. *Audit.* The Public Body, the Department of Housing and Urban Development, the Comptroller General of the United States, or any of their duly authorized representatives shall have access to any books, documents, papers, and records of the Consultant that are directly pertinent to a specific grant program for the purpose of making audit, examination, excerpts, and transcriptions.

7. *"Section 3" Compliance in the Provision of Training, Employment, and Business Opportunities:* This Agreement is subject to the requirements of Section 3 of the Housing and Urban Development Act of 1968 (12 USC 1701u) as amended, the HUD regulations issued pusuant thereto at 24 CFR Part 135, and any applicable rules and orders of HUD issued thereunder prior to the execution of this Agreement. The Section 3 clause, set forth in 24 CFR, 135.20(b) provides:

"Every applicant, recipient, contracting party, and subcontractor shall incorporate, or cause to be incorporated, in all contracts for work in connection with a Section 3 covered project, the following clause (referred to as a Section 3 clause):

A. The work to be performed under this contract is on a project assisted under a program providing direct Federal financial assistance from the Department of Housing and Urban Development and is subject to the requirements of Section 3 of the Housing and Urban Development Act of 1968, as amended, 12 USC 1701u. Section 3 requires that to the greatest extent feasible opportunities for training and employment be given lower-income residents of the project area and contracts for work in connection with the project to be awarded to business concerns which are located in, or owned in substantial part by persons residing in the area of the project.

B. The parties to the contract will comply with the provisions of said Section 3 and the regulations issued pursuant thereto by the Secretary of Housing and Urban Development set forth in 24 CFR ____, and all applicable rules and orders of the Department issued thereunder prior to the execution of this contract. The parties to the contract certify and agree that they are under no contractual or other disability which would prevent them from complying with these requirements.

C. The Contractor will send to each labor organization or representative of workers with which he has a collective bargaining agreement or other contract of understanding, if any, a notice advising the said labor organization or workers' representative of his commitments under this Section 3 clause and shall post copies of the notice in conspicuous places available to employees and applicants for employment or training.

D. The Contractor will include this Section 3 clause in every subcontract for work in connection with the project and will, at the direction of the applicant for or recipient of Federal financial assistance, take appropriate action pursuant to the subcontract upon a finding that the subcontractor is in violation of regulations issued by the Secretary of Housing and Urban Development, 24 CFR ____. The Contractor will not subcontract with any subcontractor where it has notice or knowledge that the latter has been found in violation of regulations under 24 CFR ____ and will not let any subcontract unless the subcontractor has first provided it with a preliminary statement of ability to comply with the requirements of these regulations.

E. Compliance with the provisions of Section 3, the regulations set forth in 24 CFR ____, and all applicable rules and orders of the Department issued thereunder prior to the execution of the contract shall be a condition of the Federal financial assistance provided to the project, binding upon the applicant or recipient for such assistance, its successors and assigns. Failure to fulfill these requirements shall subject the applicant or recipient, its contractors and subcontractors, its successors and assigns to those sanctions specified by the grant or loan agreement or contract through which Federal assistance is provided, and to such sanctions as are specified by 24 CFR ____.135.''

The Consultant agrees to abide by the Section 3 clause set forth above and will also cause this Section 3 clause to be inserted in any subcontracts entered into with third parties for work covered by this agreement.

8. *Equal Employment Opportunity for Activities and Contracts Not Subject to Executive Order 11246, as Amended.* In carrying out the program, the Consultant shall not discriminate against any employee or applicant for employment because of race, color, religion, sex, or national origin. The Consultant shall take affirmative action to insure that applicants for employment are employed, and that employees are treated during employment without regard to their race, color, religion, sex, or national origin. Such action shall include, but not be limited to: employment, upgrading, demotion, or transfer; recruitment or recruitment advertising; layoff or termination; rates of pay or other forms of compensation; and selection for training, including apprenticeship. The Consultant shall post in conspicuous places, available to employees and applicants for employment, notices to be provided by the Government setting forth the provisions of this nondiscrimination clause. The Consultant shall state that all qualified applicants will receive consideration for employment without regard to race, color, religion, sex, or national origin. The Consultant shall incorporate the foregoing requirements of this paragraph in all subcontracts for program work.

9. *Compliance with Air and Water Acts.* This Agreement is subject to the requirements of the Clean Air Act, as amended, 42 USC 1857 et seq., the Federal Water Pollution Control Act, as amended, 33 USC 1251 et seq., and the regulations of the Environmental Protection Agency with respect thereto, at 40 CFR Part 15, as amended from time to time.

The Contractor and any of its subcontractors for work funded under this Agreement, in excess of $100,000, agree to the following requirements:

1. A stipulation by the contractor or subcontractors that any facility to be utilized in the performance of any nonexempt contract or subcontract is not listed on the List of Violating Facilities issued by the Environmental Protection Agency (EPA) pursuant to 40 CFR 15.20.

2. Agreement by the contractor to comply with all the requirements of Section 114 of the Clean Air Act, as amended (42 USC 1857c-8) and Section 308 of the Federal Water Pollution Control Act, as amended (33 USC 1318)

relating to inspection, monitoring, entry, reports and information, as well as all other requirements specified in said Section 114 and Section 308, and all regulations and guidelines issued thereunder.

3. A stipulation that as a condition for the award of the contract prompt notice will be given of any notification received from the Director, Office of Federal Activities, EPA, indicating that a facility utilized or to be utilized for the contract is under consideration to be listed on the EPA List of Violating Facilities.

4. Agreement by the Contractor that he will include or cause to be included the criteria and requirements in paragraphs (1) through (4) of this section in every nonexempt subcontract and requiring that the contractor will take such action as the Government may direct as a means of enforcing such provision. In no event shall any amount of the assistance provided under this Agreement be utilized with respect to a facility which has given rise to a conviction under Section 113(c)(1) of the Clean Air Act or Section 309(c) of the Federal Water Pollution Control Act.

**10.** *Interest of Certain Federal Officials.* No member of or Delegate to the Congress of the United States and no Resident Commissioner shall be admitted to any share or part of this Agreement or to any benefit to arise from the same.

**11.** *Interest of Members, Officers, or Employees of Public Body, Member of Local Governing Body, or Other Public Officials.* No member, officer, or employee of the Public Body, or its designees or agents, no member of the governing body of the locality in which the program is situated, and no other public official of such locality or localities who exercises any functions or responsibilities with respect to the program during his tenure or for one year thereafter shall have any interest, direct or indirect, in any contract or subcontract, or the proceeds thereof, for work to be performed in connection with the program assisted under the Agreement.

**12.** *Prohibition against Payments of Bonus of Commission.* The assistance provided under this Agreement shall not be used in the payment of any bonus or commission for the purpose of obtaining HUD approval of the application for such assistance, or HUD approval of applications for additional assistance, or any other approval or concurrence of HUD required under this Agreement, Title I of the Housing and Community Development Act of 1974 or HUD regulations with respect thereto: provided, however, that reasonable fees or bona fide technical, consultant, managerial, or other such services, other than actual solicitation, are not hereby prohibited if otherwise eligible as program costs.

## FUND-RAISING AGREEMENT

Agreement dated _____, 198__, between _____, hereinafter referred to as the Consultant, and The _____ Foundation, Inc., a nonprofit corporation organized and existing under the laws of the State of _____, hereinafter referred to as The Foundation.

    The parties hereto agree as follows:

I. *Term*

    This Agreement shall be effective for a term of two years, commencing on the date hereof, and shall be renewed automatically from year to year thereafter unless cancelled by either of the parties hereto upon written notice given not less than 60 days prior to the termination of the contract year. This Agreement may be terminated for cause on 90 days' written notice.

*Services; Independent Contractor*

A. The Foundation hereby retains the Consultant and the Consultant hereby agrees to work for The Foundation as an independent contractor to raise funds for the Foundation subject to the terms and conditions hereinafter specified. This Agreement shall not be considered to be a partnership or joint venture. The Consultant shall exercise control over the means and manner in which he performs any work requested by The Foundation hereunder, subject to the approval of The Foundation as set forth herein.

B. The Consultant shall conduct and manage a national fund-raising and promotional campaign to help The Foundation effectuate its charitable purposes and goals and, more specifically, to help collect $_____ to be used for _____. The Consultant shall be the sole authorized outside fund raiser during the term of this Agreement.

C. The Consultant may represent other organizations and individuals, so long as such representation and/or clients are not in conflict with the aims and purposes of The Foundation and its fund-raising campaigns. The Consultant shall not be required to devote his entire time and attention to the representation of The Foundation. The Consultant further agrees that he is able and will continue to be able to represent the interests of The Foundation ably and diligently throughout the term of this Agreement and that he will do so.

III. *Compensation; Expenses*

    A. For all work performed during the original term of this Agreement. The Foundation will pay the Consultant a one-time fee of $_____ plus _____% of all contributions obtained by the Consultant that are accepted by The Foundation. During any renewal period, The Foundation will pay the Consultant _____% of all contributions obtained by the Consultant that are accepted by The Foundation.

    B. The Consultant will pay and be solely responsible for all costs and disbursements incurred in the fund-raising campaign, including but not limited to printing, reproduction services, general office supplies, and travel.

    C. The Consultant shall deliver an itemized statement to The Foundation on a monthly basis that shows fully the work being performed under this Agreement, together with all contributions received by the Consultant on behalf of The Foundation. The Foundation will pay the Consultant _____% of all contributions accepted by it within thirty (30) days of the receipt of the itemized statement together with all contributions received by the Consultant. The payment so made shall be subject to correction and to refund of overpayments and payments of deficiencies upon final acceptance or rejection of individual contributions by The Foundation.

    D. The one-time fee of $_____ shall be paid to the Consultant in four equal installments at six-month intervals from the signing of this Agreement.

    E. All contributions solicited by the Consultant are subject to final acceptance by The Foundation. The Foundation retains the right to refuse contribution in its sole discretion, and any contribution and its source are subject to investigation by The Foundation prior to their final acceptance.

IV. *Coordination; Reports*

    A. All coordination and decisions involved with the operation of the overall fund-raising and promotional campaign will be carried out by the Consultant working directly with The Foundation's appointed representative, who has full authority from The Foundation's Board of Directors to coordinate the operation of the campaign with the Consultant. All presentations, promotional materials, etc., must be approved in advance by The Foundation for accuracy, taste, and quality. It is understood and agreed the Consultant shall use only first-quality materials.

B. The Consultant will meet periodically with The Foundation to report on fund raising and the development of fund-raising prospects and he will provide, when requested, a written report of his activities for the use of The Foundation.

C. The Foundation, its officers, and directors will provide the maximum cooperation possible to assist the Consultant in raising funds on behalf of The Foundation and any expenses or disbursements incurred in assisting the Consultant hereunder at his request will be paid by the Consultant.

D. Any and all promotional materials, manuscripts, or any other work product, whether completed or not, which are prepared or developed by the Consultant as part of the work under this Agreement, shall be the exclusive property of The Foundation and shall be turned over to The Foundation promptly at The Foundation's request or at the termination of this Agreement, whichever is earlier. The Foundation shall have the exclusive right to copyright or otherwise register such materials, manuscripts, and other work products.

V. *Confidential Information*

The Consultant agrees that during the terms of this Agreement and for five years thereafter he shall not disclose or allow to be disclosed to any person, firm, or corporation any confidential information regarding The Foundation, whether related to its finances, personnel, or otherwise, including but not limited to contributors to or practices of The Foundation, without the express written consent of The Foundation.

VI. *Assignable; Subcontracts*

A. The Consultant shall have the right to assign this Agreement and the benefits subject to the obligations thereof, in whole or in part, to any person, firm, or corporation of equal responsibility with the prior written consent of The Foundation, provided, however, that the Consultant shall at all times remain liable hereon to The Foundation. Any other assignment shall terminate this Agreement and the Consultant shall be paid all money owed him as of that date.

B. The Consultant shall be permitted to hire and/or subcontract to other representatives in his capacity as an independent contractor, but he, and not The Foundation, is solely responsible for all contractual arrangements with such parties, including supervision, reimbursement for their activities, and maintenance of adequate records.

VII. *Indemnification*

The Consultant shall indemnify, defend, and hold The Foundation harmless from any and all claims, demands, suits, liabilities, judgments, and expenses (including reasonable attorney fees) asserted against The Foundation as a result of any act of the Consultant not authorized by The Foundation.

VIII. *Arbitration*

Any controversy or claim arising out of or relating to this Agreement or the breach thereof shall be settled at _____, _____, in accordance with the rules then obtaining of the American Arbitration Association, and judgment upon the award may be entered in any court having jurisdiction thereof.

IX. *Entire Agreement*

This instrument contains the entire agreement of the parties and may not be changed orally. Any modification or waiver of the terms of this Agreement must be in writing, duly executed by both parties.

IN WITNESS WHEREOF, the parties have hereunto set their hands and seals and caused these presents to be executed by their appropriate corporate officers as of the date first above written.

_____            THE _____ FOUNDATION, INC.

By_____            By _____
                                                                                President

Witness:                                                    Attest:

_____            _____
                                                                                Secretary

## ARBITRATION CLAUSES

For the arbitration of future disputes, the American Arbitration Association recommends the following arbitration clause for insertion in all commercial contracts:

"Any controversy or claim arising out of or relating to this contract, or the breach thereof, shall be settled by arbitration in accordance with the Commercial Arbitration Rules of the American Arbitration Association, and judgment upon the award rendered by the Arbitrator(s) may be entered in any Court having jurisdiction thereof."

This clause is recommended for the submission of existing disputes:

"We, the undersigned parties, hereby agree to submit to arbitration under the Commercial Arbitration Rules of the American Arbitration Association the following controversy: (cite briefly). We further agree that the above controversy be submitted to (one) (three) Arbitrator(s) selected from the panels of Arbitrators of the American Arbitration Association. We further agree that we will faithfully observe this agreement and the Rules and that we will abide by and perform any award rendered by the Arbitrator(s) and that a judgment of the Court having jurisdiction may be entered upon the award."

# EXTRACTS FROM *A Commercial Arbitration Guide for Business People,* BY THE AMERICAN ARBITRATION ASSOCIATION

## CHECKLIST FOR INITIATING ARBITRATION

|  | **By Demand for Arbitration** | **By Submission Agreement** |
|---|---|---|
| Disposition of Original | Mailed to respondent. | Filed with AAA in duplicate. |
| Copies Needed by AAA | Two. | Two. |
| Copies Retained by Parties | Demanding party retains one. | Each party retains one. |
| Signature Required | Authorized person for demanding party, signature and title. | Authorized persons for both parties, signatures and titles. |
| Identification of Parties | Responding party should be clearly identified by official name and address. | Official names and addresses of both parties should appear, with signatures and titles. |
| Contract Clauses | Arbitration clause should be quoted in full. (May be attached separately if more convenient.) Include date of document. | Not applicable. |
| Administrative Fee | Must be advanced by demanding party. Arbitrators later apportion fees. See schedule on page 14. | May be shared equally. Arbitrator later apportions fees. See schedule on page 14. |
| Statement of Dispute | Should be brief but clear and include amount claimed, if any, and relief sought. | Claim and answer should be brief but clear and include amount claimed, if any, and relief sought. |
| Answering Statement | Respondent may mail answering statement to claimant and file two copies with AAA. | See above. |
| Composition of Arbitration Board | AAA will determine number of arbitrators unless composition is stated in arbitration clause. | Number of arbitrators desired may be stated. If not stated, AAA will determine composition of board. |
| Locale of Arbitration | If not provided for in arbitration clause, demanding party should indicate preference. | Should be indicated, if possible. |

# American Arbitration Association

**COMMERCIAL ARBITRATION RULES**
**DEMAND FOR ARBITRATION**

DATE: March 16, 1979

TO: (Name) ACME IMPORTING COMPANY
(of party upon whom the Demand is made)

(Address) 4071 West Street

(City and State) Chicago, Ill.      (Zip Code) 60601

(Telephone)

Named claimant, a party to an arbitration agreement contained in a written contract,

dated November 17, 1978 , providing for arbitration, hereby demands arbitration thereunder.
(attach arbitration clause or quote hereunder)

Any controversy or claim arising out of or relating to this contract, or any breach thereof, shall be settled in accordance with the Rules of the American Arbitration Association, and judgment upon the award may be entered in any Court having jurisdiction thereof.

NATURE OF DISPUTE:

Claimant alleges breach of contract on the part of Acme Importing Company in that shipment of 407 bales of jute was not of first grade quality, as required by the contract dated November 17, 1978.

CLAIM OR RELIEF SOUGHT: (amount, if any)

An allowance of $60 per bale is demanded, to a total of $24,420.

HEARING LOCALE REQUESTED:      Chicago, Illinois
(City and State)

You are hereby notified that copies of our arbitration agreement and of this demand are being filed with the American Arbitration Association at its Chicago Regional Office, with the request that it commence the administration of the arbitration. Under Section 7 of the Commercial Arbitration Rules, you may file an answering statement within seven days after notice from the Administrator.

Signed *Joseph Harriman*      Title President
(May be Signed by Attorney)

Name of Claimant The Hanover Burlap Company

Address (to be used in connection with this case) 4100 Claremont Avenue

City and State Chicago, Ill.   Zip Code 60601

Telephone

Name of Attorney Thomas J. Lyons

Address 113 East Street

City and State Chicago, Ill.   Zip Code 60601

Telephone

To institute proceedings, please send three copies of this Demand with the administrative fee, as provided in Section 48 of the Rules, to the AAA. Send original Demand to Respondent.

FORM C2-AAA

# American Arbitration Association

### SUBMISSION TO ARBITRATION

Date:  August 6, 1979

The named Parties hereby submit the following dispute to arbitration under the COMMERCIAL ARBITRATION RULES of the American Arbitration Association:

Under lease dated January 1, 1978, Bricker Realty Company demands payment of $1,248 in rental, such sum representing 10 percent of the charges made to customers of Rotary Clothes for alterations on garments bought during the first six months of 1979.  Rotary Clothes contests this demand, claiming that alterations performed by subcontracting tailor are not "gross sales" within the meaning of said lease and are therefore not subject to rental fees.

Amount of money involved:  $1,248

Number of Arbitrators desired:  one ☒  three ☐

Place of Hearing:  Chicago, Illinois

We agree that we will abide by and perform any Award rendered hereunder and that a judgment may be entered upon the Award.

Name of Party    Bricker Realty Company

Address    177 S. LaSalle St., Chicago, Ill.

Signed by *Harold T. Burnett* , Attorney

Name of Party    Rotary Clothes, Inc.

Address    147 W. Monroe St., Chicago, Ill.

Signed by *Sam Miller* , President

PLEASE FILE TWO COPIES
Consult counsel about valid execution

FORM AAA-C1

PROCEDURE FOR ORAL HEARINGS

| | Who Decides | Who Makes Arrangements | Notice |
|---|---|---|---|
| Time | The arbitrator, at the convenience of the parties. | Tribunal administrator, who consults the parties and arbitrator. | At least five days given by tribunal administrator unless parties agree otherwise. |
| Representation by Counsel | The individual party. | The individual party. | Three days' notice to other party unless arbitration was initiated by counsel, in which case notice is deemed to have been given. |
| Stenographic Record and Interpreters | The individual party. | The tribunal adminstrator. | Not necessary, but the tribunal administrator may inquire of the other side as to whether it would like to share the cost and get a copy of the record. |
| Attendance at Hearing | Parties attend and bring witnesses. Arbitrator may decide what other interested persons may attend and may require withdrawal of witnesses during the testimony of others. | Parties arrange for attendance of witnesses. | Parties notify their own interested persons. |

| | | | |
|---|---|---|---|
| Affidavits and Documents | The arbitrator decides whether to receive such evidence when it is presented. | Each party arranges to submit its own documents. If they are in the possession of the other party, documents may be requested directly. | None required. |
| Subpoena of Witnesses and Documents | Arbitrator issues subpoena on showing of need by a party. | Tribunal administrator obtains signature of arbitrator for subpoena supplied by party and returns subpoena to party for service. | Subpoena is served by parties directly on witness or custodian of documents. |
| Inspection or Investigation | Arbitrator may decide on his or her own initiative or at the request of a party, if the arbitrator deems it necesary. | Tribunal administrator. | Parties are notified of time and place of inspection so that they may be present. |
| Close of Oral Hearings | Arbitrator closes hearing after both sides complete proofs and witnesses. If briefs, investigation or more data are required, hearings are kept open. | Tribunal administrator arranges for receipt of post-hearing matters and makes a record of close of hearings on instructions from arbitrator. | Tribunal administrator notifies parties of all official closing dates. |

## BASIC REFERENCES

### American Arbitration Association Regional Offices

100 Peachtree Street, N.W., Atlanta, Georgia 30303
294 Washington Street, Boston, Massachusetts 02106
3235 Eastway Drive, P.O. Box 18951, Charlotte, South Carolina 28218
180 North La Salle Street, Chicago, Illinois 60601
2308 Carew Tower, Cincinnati, Ohio 45202
215 Euclid Avenue, Cleveland, Ohio 44114
1607 Main Street, Dallas, Texas 75201
1234 City National Bank Building, Detroit, Michigan 48226
585 Stewart Avenue, Garden City, New York 11530
37 Lewis Street, Hartford, Connecticut 06103
443 Shatto Place, Los Angeles, California 90020
2250 S.W. Third Avenue, Miami, Florida 33129
1001 Foshay Tower, Minneapolis, Minnesota 55402
96 Bayard Street, New Brunswick, New Jersey 08901
140 West 51st Street, New York, New York 10020
1521 Locust Street, Philadelphia, Pennsylvania 19102
222 North Central Avenue, Phoenix, Arizona 85004
221 Gateway Four, Pittsburgh, Pennsylvania 15222
530 Broadway, San Diego, California 92101
445 Bush Street, San Francisco, California 94108
810 Third Avenue, Seattle, Washington 98104
731 James Street, Syracuse, New York 13203
1730 Rhode Island Avenue, N.W., Washington, D.C. 20036
24 South Broadway, White Plains, New York 10601

### Consultant Organizations

American Association of Fund-Raising Counsel, Inc.
500 Fifth Avenue
New York, N.Y. 10036

American Consulting Engineers Council
Suite 802, 1015 15th Street, N.W.
Washington, D.C. 20005

American Council of Independent Laboratories, Inc.
1725 K Street, N.W.
Washington, D.C. 20006

American Institute of Architects
1735 New York Avenue, N.W.
Washington, D.C. 20006

American Management Associations
135 West 50th Street
New York, N.Y. 10020

The American Marketing Association
222 South Riverside Plaza
Chicago, Illinois 60606

American Society of Agricultural Consultants
Enterprise Center
Suite 470, 8301 Greensboro Drive
McLean, Virginia 22102

American Society of Appraisers
P.O. Box 17265
Washington, D.C. 20041

Association of Consulting Chemists and Chemical Engineers
Suite 92, 50 East 41st Street
New York, N.Y. 10017

Association of Consulting Management Engineers, Inc.
230 Park Avenue
New York, N.Y. 10017

Association of Executive Recruiting Consultants, Inc.
Suite 1914, 30 Rockefeller Plaza
New York, N.Y. 10112

Association of Graphic Arts Consultants
1730 North Lynn Street
Arlington, Virginia 22209

Association of Productivity Specialists
Pan Am Building
Suite 303E, 200 Park Avenue
New York, N.Y. 10017

Independent Computer Consultants Association
P.O. Box 27412
St. Louis, Missouri 63141

Institute of Management Consultants, Inc.
19 West 44th Street
New York, N.Y. 10036

Institute of Management Consultants, Inc.
347 Madison Avenue
New York, N.Y. 10017

National Association of Freight Transportation Consultants
14 Station Road
Simsbury, Connecticut 06070

National Association of Merger & Acquisition Consultants
2241 Valwood Parkway
Dallas, Texas 75234

National Society of Professional Engineers
2029 K Street, N.W.
Washington, D.C. 20006

Society of Professional Management Consultants
205 West 89th Street
New York, N.Y. 10024

Society of Telecommunications Consultants
Suite 1912, One Rockefeller Plaza
New York, N.Y. 10020

## Publications

DIRECTORIES
*Bradford's Directory of Marketing Research Agencies and Management Consultants in the United States and the World*

Bradford's Directory of Marketing Research Agencies
P.O. Box 276
Fairfax, Virginia 20030

*Consultants and Consulting Organizations Directory*
*Encyclopedia of Organizations*

Gale Research
Book Tower
Detroit, Michigan 48226

*Consultants Directory*

Harris / Ragan Management Corporation
9200 Sunset Boulevard
Los Angeles, California 90069

*Directory of Management Consultants*

Consultants News
Templeton Road
Fitzwilliam, New Hampshire 03447

*Directory of Personal Image Consultants*

Editorial Services Company
1140 Avenue of the Americas
10th Floor
New York, N.Y. 10036

*The Forensic Services Directory*

National Forensic Center
6 Ashburn Place
Fair Lawn, N.J. 07410

*National Trade and Professional Associations of the U.S. and Labor Unions*

Columbia Books, Inc.
734 15th Street, N.W.
Washington, D.C. 20005

*Scientific and Technical Societies of the U.S.*

National Academy of Sciences
Washington, D.C. 20418

PERIODICALS
*Boardroom Reports*

Boardroom Reports, Inc.
500 Fifth Avenue
New York, N.Y. 10710

Contains brief notes on current management issues, including use of management consultants. The notes lead the subscriber to books, periodicals, and businesses for further advice.

*Commerce Business Daily*

Superintendent of Documents
Government Printing Office
Washington, D.C. 20402

The official listing of all government contracts, including consulting assignments, put out for public bidding.

*Consultants News*

Info Co.
Box 35
Norwood, New Jersey 07648

A newsletter aimed at those in management consulting, including personnel recruitment.

REFERENCES
Altman, M. A., and Weil, R. J., *Managing Your Accounting and Consulting Practice* (1978)

Matthew Bender
235 East 45th Street
New York, N.Y. 10017

Outlines consultant practices on accounting, fees and billing.

Bell, C. R., *The Client Consultant Handbook* (1979)

Gulf Publishing Company
Box 2608
Houston, Texas 77001

Explores psychological elements of the client-consultant relationship.

Shay, P. W., *How To Get The Best Results From Management Consultants* (1974)

Association of Consulting Management Engineers, Inc.
347 Madison Avenue
New York, N.Y. 10017

An association-printed booklet, concentrating on management consultants.

Webster, G. D., *The Law of Associations* (1979)

Matthew Bender
235 East 45th Street
New York, N.Y. 10017

A legal reference work on the legal powers and limitations on trade of professional associations.


## The U.S. Government and Consultants

GENERAL REFERENCE
Holtz, Herman, *The $100 Billion Market* (1980)

AMACOM
135 W. 50th Street
New York, N.Y. 10020

Information on doing business with the government, including as a consultant.

U.S. GENERAL ACCOUNTING OFFICE

"Improvements and New Legislation Needed in AID's Contracting for Consultants and Advisors" (ID-76-82, Dec. 27, 1970)

"Government Consultants: Standard Definition and Uniform Data Needed" (FPCD-78-5, Nov. 29, 1977)

"Controls Over Consulting Service Contracts at Federal Agencies Need Tightening" (PSAD-80-35, March 20, 1980)

"Government Earns Low Marks on Proper Use of Consultants" (FPCD-80-48, June 5, 1980)

U.S. SENATE

"Consultants and Contractors," U.S. Senate Committee on Governmental Affairs, Subcommittee on Reports, Accounting and Management, 95th Congress, 1st Session, August 1977.

"Development of a Uniform Reporting System for Federal Consultants and Contractors," Hearings Before the U.S. Senate Committee on Governmental Affairs, Subcommittee on Reports, Accounting and Management, 95th Congress, 1st Session, Sept. 1977.

"Federal Government's Use of Consultant Services," Hearings Before the U.S. Senate Committee on Governmental Affairs, Subcommittee on Civil Services and General Services, 96th Congress, 1st Session, Oct. 1979.

"Federal Consulting Service Contracts," Joint Hearing Before the U.S. Senate Committee on Governmental Affairs, Subcommittee on Civil Service and General Services, and U.S. House of Representatives Committee on Post Office and Civil Service, Subcommittee on Human Resources, 96th Congress, 2nd Session, Pt. 1, March–April, 1980.

# INDEX

Academics, 3
Accountants, outside independent public, 50
Acquisitions, 48–50
American Arbitration Association (AAA), 91, 131–134
Appraisal and review form, 59–60, 65–68
Arbitration, 91–92, 120, 130–134
  reasons for use of, 131–132
Assignability, 75, 89–91, 114–116

Bidding, competitive, 11
Billing, 41–43, 63–65, 85, 101–105
Billing statements, 64–65, 104–105
Breach of contract, 125–131
"Bucket shop" operators, 49
Budget clause, in corporate policy, 60–61
Budgeting, 32–34
Budget review, 54, 55, 57, 61

Cancellation option, 74, 114
Compensation, 73, 84–85, 97, 101–103
  See also Fees
Confidential information, 37–40, 62, 74, 88–89, 106–108
Conflicts of interest, 34–35, 54, 58, 59, 74, 117
Consultants (consulting)
  definitions of, 2–6, 9, 10, 55–56
  determination of need for, 10–13
  diversity of, 2
  finding, 18–29
  legal perspective on, 4–5
  management perspective on, 2–4

reasons for using, 4, 12
selection of, 13–15, 36–37
task of, definition of, 13–15
traps to avoid, 12–13, 15
See also specific topics
Consultant organizations, 19–29
  complaints to, 22–23, 27–29
  dispute resolution and, 22–23, 28–29
  ethical standards and, 22–23, 27–29
  forms, standard and suggested, 22–23, 25–27
  membership qualifications of, 20–24
  referrals and placement and, 22–25
Consulting agreement, 6–10, 70
  disputes and, 124, 125, 130–131 (see also Breach of contract)
  drafting of, 70–76
    applicable law, 75–76
    compensation, 73
    copyrights, 72
    costs, 73
    duration, 73–74
    independent contractor status, 72
    modification, 75
    nonassignability, 75
    patents, 72
    restrictive covenants, 74–75
    services to be performed, 70–72
    termination, 74
    termination notice, 76
    work product, right to obtain, 72
  letter. See Letter agreement
  modifications of, 9, 34, 92, 75, 120

Consulting agreement (*continued*)
oral, 8, 10, 49
renewal of, 8, 74
rescission of, 127
review, 54–55, 57, 58
standard form, 25–27
statute of frauds and, 8
*See also* Contracts
Continuing basis, retention on, 83, 84, 89
Contractor, independent, 6–9, 35–36, 70–72, 87, 111
Contracts, 61, 70, 71
breach of, 125–131
confidential information and, 38–40
difference between letter agreement and, 78
elaborate, 96
form, 25–27, 96–97
master. *See* Master consulting contract
modification of, 34, 120
personal services, 75, 128–129, 131
recruitment of consultant's employees and, 39–40
recruitment of corporate employees and, 39
specialized, 122
*See also* Consulting agreement
Copyrights, 72, 105–106, 109
Corporate opportunities, 117
Corporate policy, 46–68
centralized, 68
on conflicts of interest, 34–35, 54, 58
decentralized, 54–61
other existing, consultants and, 47–54
conflicts of interest, 54, 58
finder's fees, 48–50
Foreign Corrupt Policies Act, 53
insider trading, 52–53
outside independent public accountants, 50
outside legal counsel and lobbyists, 51–52
references, 53–54
risk management, 52
sample, 54–61
alternative, 68
coverage, 55–56
limitations on use of consultants, 56–57
optional provisions, 58–61
prior approval, 57–58
topics covered by, 46–47
United States Department of Health and Human Services, 33–34
written, reasons for, 46
Cost-plus-percentage contracts, 97, 102

Costs (expenses), 73, 84–85, 101–105
insurance, 118
legal, 108–110
*See also* Disbursements

Damages
liquidated, 130–131
suit for, 126–127
Directories, consultant-organization, 24–25
Disbursements, 43–44
Discrimination, 112–113
Disputes, 28–29, 97, 119–120, 124–134
arbitration of, 91–92, 120, 130–134
causes of, 124
handling of, 124–126
lawsuits and, 126–129
mediation of, 129–130
remedies provided by agreement, 130–131
Duration clauses, 73–74, 80–81

Employment contract, 6, 7, 75
Encyclopedia of Organizations, 19
Equal employment opportunity, 112–113
Equitable remedies, 126, 127

Fees
consulting, 40–44, 73, 84, 101, 102
finder's, 48–50
Fidelity bonds, 37
Final report, 58–59, 67
Finder's fees, 48–50
"Fly-by-night" operators, 49
Foreign Corrupt Practices Act, 53, 58
Forms, standard, 25–27
Fraud, 37
Frauds, statute of, 8, 9, 55, 73, 75, 120
Fund-raising consultant, 122

Good faith, 124–125
Government, 2–5, 56–57

Health and Human Services, United States Department of, 33–34, 68
Housing and Urban Development, United States Department of, 122

Indemnifications, 108, 109
Independent-contractor relationship, 6–9, 35–36, 70–72, 87, 111
Information, confidential, 37–40, 62, 74, 88–89, 106–108
Insurance, 35–37, 52, 110, 118
Integration clauses, 92, 96, 121

Justice, United States Department of, 29

Law firm, fees of, 40–44
Lawsuits, 126–129
Legal counsel, outside, 51
Legal issues, 4–10, 70–76
  *See also* Indemnifications; Liability
Legal review, 55, 57
Letter agreements, 61, 70, 78–93, 96
  adaptation to particular needs, 79–93
  arbitration and, 91–92
  closing of, 92–93
  compensation and expenses, 84–85
  confidentiality of information, 88–89
  difference between contract and, 78
  duration of appointment, 80–81
  independent contractor status, 87
  integration clause, 92
  nature of services, 81–83, 93
  nonassignability of, 89–91
  progress of work, 84
  reports and work products, 86–87
  termination of, 88
  working facilities, 85–86
  written, 78–79
Liability, 51, 53, 72, 109
  limitations of, 110–111, 115
  vicarious, 6, 9
Liability insurance, 36–37
Licensing, 24
Liquidated damages, 130–131
Lobbyists, 51–52

Master consulting contract, 96–122
  adaptation of form, 96–97
  amendments to, 120
  applicable law, 119
  assignability of, 114–116
  billing procedure, 103–105
  compensation and costs, 101–103
  confidential information, 106–108
  conflicts of interest, 117
  corporate opportunities, 117
  disputes and arbitration, 119–120
  equal employment opportunity, 112–113
  indemnifications, 108, 109
  independent contractor status, 111
  insurance, 118
  integration clause, 121
  liability, limitations of, 108
  notices, 111–112
  parties, 98

patents and copyrights, 105–106
scope of work, 98–99
severability clause, 121–122
subcontractors and employers, 116–117
termination of, 113–114
waivers, 120–121
work product, 105
work requests, 99–101
Mediation, 129–130
Mergers, 48–50
Modifications of agreement, 9, 34, 75, 92, 100, 120
"Motherhood" statement, 58

National Council of Professional Services Firms, 19–20
Nepotism, 35
Nonassignment clauses, 75, 89–91, 115
Noncompete clause, 117, 129
Noncompetitive covenants, 74–75
Notices, 111–112
  termination, 76

Office of Education, United States, 99
Office of Management and Budget, United States, 56–57
Oral agreement, 8, 10, 49, 79
Oral modification, 75, 92, 120
Overseas consultants, 53, 58

Patents, 72, 105–106
Personal services contract, 75, 128–129, 131
Prepackaged solutions, 15

Records, 72
  employee, 53
  *See also* Reports; Work papers
Recruitment
  of consultant's employees, 39–40
  of corporate employees, 39
References, 53–54
Relatives, employment of, 35
Renewal of agreement, 8, 74
Reports (reporting), 15, 86–87
  final, 58–59, 67
Request for a Proposal (RFP), 11, 14
Rescission, 127
Restitution, 127
Restrictive covenants, 74–75
Retention form, 59–62, 66
Retention letter, sample, 62–63

Review
  budget and contract, 54–55, 57, 58, 61
  form, appraisal and, 56–60, 65–68
  legal, 55, 57
RFP (Request for a Proposal), 11, 14
Risk management, 35–37, 52

Secrets
  business, 107, 108
  *See also* Confidential information
Securities, insider trading of, 52–53
Securities and Exchange Commission (SEC), 50
Services to be performed (task), definition of, 13–15, 70–72, 81–83, 93, 98–99
Severability clause, 121–122
Similar work clause, 60
Specific performance remedy, 128–129, 131
Stocks, insider trading of, 52–53
Subcontracting, 115–117

Termination of agreement, 74, 88, 113–114
  notice of, 76
Theft, 37

Time for performance
  definition of, 71–72, 98
  *See also* Duration clauses
Time period, retention for specific, 80
Time records, 41–42
Trademarks, 108
Trade secrets, 108, 109
Trading, insider, 52–53

Unsolicited proposals, 49–50

Vicarious liability, 6, 9

White-collar crime, 37
Worker's compensation coverage, 36
Working facilities (work place), 6, 85–86
Work papers
  disposition of, 14–15
  *See also* Records
Work product
  right to obtain, 72, 86–87, 105
  *See also* Records; Reports
Work requests, 98–101, 104